INSIDE BANGLADESH TODAY

INSIDE BANGLADESH TODAY

An Eye-Witness Account

BASANT CHATTERJEE

S. CHAND & CO (Pvt) LTD
RAM NAGAR, NEW DELHI-110055

S. CHAND & CO (Pvt) Ltd

H.O. : RAM NAGAR, NEW DELHI-110055
Show Room : 4/16-B, ASAF ALI ROAD, NEW DELHI-110001

Branches :

Mai Hiran Gate, Jullundur-144001
Aminabad Park, Lucknow-226001
36, Vijay Chambers,
Opposite Dreamland Cinema,
Bombay-400004

32, Ganesh Chandra Ave.,
Calcutta-700013
35, Mount Road, Madras-600002
Sultan Bazar, Hyderabad-500001
Khazanchi Road, Patna-800004

U. S. Library of Congress
Catalogue Card No. 73-906296

First Published 1973

*Published by S. Chand & Co. (Pvt.) Ltd., Ram Nagar, New Delhi-110055
and printed at Rajendra Ravindra Printers (Pvt.) Ltd., Ram Nagar,
New Delhi-110055*

Preface

Ever since the birth of Independent Bangladesh, on December 16, 1971, I had been contemplating a visit to that country to make a firsthand study of conditions there. The intention, of course, was to present, as far as possible, a factual and impartial account of those conditions, so that the Indian reading public could view the emotional upsurge that had overtaken some sections of our people over la'affaire Bangladesh, in the proper perspective. Even otherwise, such an effort was in order by way of a modest contribution to contemporary history. For, much had been said and written on this subject which needed to be gone into with an open mind.

This modest ambition was fulfilled some fifteen months later in May 1973, when I finalised my plans to spend a fortnight with the people of Bangladesh who were just beginning to recover from the devastating impact of the catastrophe. During the intervening period, the shattered country had got some respite to put itself together : a new constitution had been adopted, and elections under it had been held, the re-installed regime thus acquiring much wider legitimacy. The new government of Sheikh Mujib had now set itself on stronger foundations, with an impressive record of achievements in the very first year of its rule. As such, a sympathetic observer could entertain some hope that what he would see now in Bangladesh would not just be a picture of post-war disruption but perhaps a certain regeneration also, wherein he would be able to study some of the new social and psychological forces thrown up by liberation.

No government department, institution or affluent newspaper had underwritten the tour. Therefore, the wherewithal had to come from my own meagre resources. The reason for including this rather personal note is the necessity to raise the curtain on a somewhat delicate aspect of India-Bangladesh relations. It is this : that all the Indian newsmen and other observers who have been to Bangladesh since its coming into being 'have had to enjoy' the approval or direct patronage of the Indian Government. As such, they could hardly be expected even to observe, let alone mention, such truths about the relations between the two countries as would not be to the liking of the two governments. From that angle, I am perhaps the first Indian observer to have travelled to Bangladesh without any prior commitments, that is, with no preconceptions to prove and no ideology to serve. For this independence, or waywardness as it could be called, I had to face serious difficulties and obstacles in Bangladesh.

The account that follows is a straight reportage of my 16-day stay in Bangladesh. It cannot but be circumscribed by my own disposition and receptivity; the burden of responsibility for its content is, therefore, necessarily mine.

New Delhi,   BASANT CHATTERJEE
October 3, 1973

Contents

Acknowledgements

My foremost thanks are due to my senior colleague in the profession, Mr. Sam Castelino, Editor, *Dateline Delhi*. I owe him an unrepayable debt of gratitude for his quiet magnanimity in going through the manuscript, despite many preoccupations, and straightening out many of the kinks that would have caused confusion to the reader and embarrassment to the publishers. Next, I have to thank P.K. Banerjee for painstakingly typing out the MSS. My thanks are also due to Mir Mushtaq Ahmed, Chairman of Delhi's Metropolitan Council, for his gracious help in obtaining the passport, and to the Bangladesh High Commission for swiftly endorsing it.

Some acknowledgements are made in the body of the book in their relevant setting. The persons concerned are Mr. Girilal Jain, Resident Editor, *The Times of India*, New Delhi; Mr. Kirit Bhaumik, *The Times of India* Special Correspondent in Dacca; and Mr. Inam-ul-Haq, Principal Information Officer of Bangladesh. Each of these gentlemen, in some decisive way, lent a hand in making this study tour possible.

Finally, I thank my publishers for their promptitude in bringing out the book in record time.

B. C.

CHAPTER 1

Dacca—The Incomplete Capital

RIGHT FROM Dacca's Tejgaon Airport, a series of experiences, some good but mostly unpleasant, opens up. The first pleasing experience is that of the time taken in the scrutiny of papers on Arrival as compared to what is consumed back at Dum Dum for clearing Departure ; it appears to be no more than one-tenth of the latter. Moreover, Indian passport-holders seem to enjoy a certain partiality at the hands of the staff here—which is certainly a most gratifying experience. But that seems to be the end of the privilege. For, further on, through Exchange and the Customs, what appears to be privilege is only unbridled corruption. In Exchange, for example, an extra private discount seems to be quite in order, probably because one is invariably presumed to carry much more currency than what one declares on the form. Similarly, the Customs personnel would let go your baggage without so much as a look at it. But as you begin to move out, the porter would openly stretch his hand for what is obviously 'the pooled share', hinting at the same time that the baggage might still be carried

1

back and 're-checked'. Naturally, most of those who come to Bangladesh these days can hardly afford to ignore the implied threat. So, a standard behaviour has been established.

Outside, currency is freely exchanged. Both at the State Bank in New Delhi and among friends in Calcutta, the writer was made much fun of for having obtained a regular small exchange as per regulations. Clerks and friends were unanimous in their opinion that 'Bangladesh is a country where you can go with all the money you need right in your pocket. Still, if you fear any chance check-up, you can draw a 'secret hundi' from any trader in Calcutta. In that case, you would get 150 takas for every 100 Indian rupees, whereas the official exchange rate is only 99 for 100.'

Be that as it may, there is not the slightest doubt that illegal exchange of Indian currency is taking place in Bangladesh on a vast scale. Thousands of black-marketeers and smugglers on both sides are deeply involved in this business with the connivance of the border guards. Traders collect Indian currency at a premium of 50 to 60 per cent, use the money for buying and smuggling goods from Calcutta, and earn up to 200 per cent profit by selling those goods at four to five times the normal prices. Since, however, the goods are generally sub-standard, all that Indian industry gets in return is a bad name in this country.

Public conveyance in Dacca seems to be confined mostly to cycle-rickshaws, which may well be described as 'the representative vehicle of present-day Bangladesh'. But the fares demanded sound like those of tourist taxis in Delhi ; they make one feel very small and helpless rather than angry. Then, for no reason whatever, one is beset with sudden anxieties ; one starts running from pillar to post with a peculiar uncertainty following one all the time. While thus being pushed about in the melee, the bewildered, lonely traveller is at times seized by the strange after-thought that perhaps his coming to Bangladesh like that has been a terrible blunder after all. Perhaps the best he can do now is to board the return plane straightaway, fly home, and forget all about it ! Who knows he may finally end up by getting stranded in this stark, menacing land, a destitute. All kinds of dark thoughts invade the mind. There is too much distress and scrambling here all around ; there is fear and foreboding in every pair of eyes. The grisly hand of deprivation seems to lie on everything. Not a trace of dignity or of calm or repose can be seen anywhere. There is only want and hankering and desperation on every face. So, a bloodbath is not all that is needed for the restoration of a people's health; something else is also necessary. Whatever it is, Bangladesh has emerged without acquiring it.

Thus absorbed in philosophy at Dacca Airport, the sensitive traveller finally forms an aphorism of his own: it is easy enough to fill up bomb craters, leaving no trace of the original sin; but fissures that occur in the character of peoples over long periods of subjection are a different matter, they take an equally long time to be repaired.

But to come back to more practical things: I had distant relatives and former friends in Dacca, but didn't have any of their addresses. In fact, to trace them out was one of the purposes of my mission. However, I had a pretty long list of other addresses which I had collected from friends and relatives in Delhi and Calcutta. But these formed only a reference list, to be used only in times of dire need.

One such reference was to a high Bangladeshi officer of the Central Service of erstwhile Pakistan; he was now serving under the Bangladesh Government. It was to this officer, therefore, that I initially turned for aid and guidance, which, to my immense relief, I received in ample measure. And thus my first three days in Dacca were taken care of by the homely hospitality of this unassuming and large-hearted gentleman.

Today in this city, and presumably throughout Bangladesh, the language and script of all signboards is strictly Bengali. All vehicle numberplates too are in Bengali numerals. Let alone Urdu, even English seems to have fallen in virtual disuse. Purely English words, such as 'Inter-Continental', etc., are inscribed only in blazing Bengali letters—which transliteration renders them rather difficult to make out at first sight. Hundreds of English terms seem to have been literally translated, and the translations too are often so high-flown and Sanskritised that even Bengali-knowing persons would find them hard to digest.

Seeing such a profusion of Bengali lettering everywhere and the obvious emphasis and enthusiasm in their use, the thoughtful visitor is naturally led to musing on several problems: Does this

Sanskritised Bengali happen to be the only basis for the people of this country to build their edifice of separate nationhood ? And if this is the only basis, then how are they going to differentiate and distinguish their new-found nationalism from the older and more powerful sub-nationalism of our Bengal, which too draws most of its strength and sustenance from this rich language, though not exclusively based on it ? Would the people of Bangladesh go in for a different kind of social and economic system so as to bring about the kind of differentiation that divides, say, the two parts of Germany ? Or, would they, after experimenting with borrowed ideas, come back to that one basis of their existence which is the only point of difference between them and the bulk of the Indians, and on the strength of which, indeed, they had separated in 1947 ? Supposing, on the contrary, they come to lose whatever sense of separateness they have acquired through living in Pakistan, what would then be the likely result of further strengthening of those ties of language, race, and geography which bind them to us ?

Satisfactory answers to all these questions did finally present themselves to the writer during his 16-day stay in Bangladesh, and it is precisely to set forth these answers in a reasoned and convincing manner that I have made bold to write this series of works.

Another feature of the city that hits you in the eye is the incompleteness of, and apparent suspension of work halfway on, most of the modern buildings in the new part. This state of affairs is

particularly evident in the prestigious locality called
the Motijheel Commercial Area. It is a well laid-
out, small complex of impressive, multistorey
buildings, patterned around spacious round-abouts
with inter-linking networks of fairly wide streets.
Yet as you look up, your eyes meet with bare concrete columns standing forlornly on the top roofs
of most buildings, with the steel bars protruding
out of them like stalks of some strange growth.
The naked columns are blackened and disfigured
by the eroding effects of successive monsoons, and
the iron bars, now all twisted and tangled, are
covered with deep layers of rust.

The condition of the streets below is much the
same. Many a round-about is nothing more than a
mound of raw earth and vegetation, no brick-lining
having ever been undertaken. Footpaths run for
some distance, then end abruptly, with only mud
and pot-holes for the rest of the way. In many
places, the roads are where people just walk, turning
the strips of bare earth into muddy tracks.

I was told that this sorry shape of things had
existed since a particular date towards the end of
1969, which was one of the unfortunate days in the
history of erstwhile Pakistan. On that day, the
former President Ayub Khan had stepped down,
a sober man, handing over the reins of power to his
C-in-C, Yahya Khan. Since all this building activity
was going on under the personal care and benevo-
lence of Ayub Khan, the coming of Yahya naturally
put a halt to it under the new pressure of events.
It is from that time that this unfortunate situation
has obtained in the heart of new Dacca. And it

invariably depresses and disheartens every sensitive visitor who likes to see things in their whole.

The present Mujib Government is understandably too preoccupied with averting the threat of famine and repairing the ravages of war and despoliation to find time or resources to attend to the unfinished task. Thus, on the very first day, the deepest impression the city makes on a visitor is that of a national capital which (like the state power it symbolises, as it turned out later) is destined to remain incomplete and unsatisfactory for many years to come.

———————

CHAPTER 2

The City and its People—Where are the Bhadraloks ?

RESIDENTIAL HOUSES in today's Dacca present a colourful appearance—but in a different light. The outer walls of most houses, particularly those with wide facades, are covered from top to bottom with political slogans. These were apparently put there by the workers of the various political parties during the election campaign early this year. And there they remain ever since, in anticipation of the rains.

At places the calligraphy is really artistic. But, as a rule, only roughly-shaped, large Bengali letters are drawn in diverse colours—red, blue, black, green. The number and diversity of these lines of writing is astounding. Seeing them in such abundance all over the city, one is naturally led to marvel at the courage and diligent labour of those thousands of literate workers who must have used tall ladders, or possibly hung themselves down from the parapets, to do all that writing. The inmates of these houses too seem to deserve credit for the patience, tolerance and patriotism they have apparently shown in putting up with all this violation of their privacy. In any case, the result is that houses in Dacca are at present very much disfigured, and nobody seems to bother about having them re-whitewashed. Perhaps the fear is that no sooner a fresh coat of lime is put on them than the political workers will reappear on the scene and cover the walls with the stale slogans all over again. So, why not wait for the rains?

People in the know say that in Bangladesh today, the second largest field of employment, after agriculture, happens to be politics. This, of course, is an exaggeration. But there is no doubt that thousands of young men in this much politics-ridden country are now earning their daily bread through politics. As things are, this cannot but lead to unprecedented inflation.

Notable buildings in new Dacca are not many, and the few that merit mention are all concentrated in a small area known loosely as Motijheel. Till 1958, it is said, this entire area was mostly jungle and marsh; even today there are village-like settlements within the area, where one can see regular agriculture being practised. On its eastern end now stands the new railway station of Dacca, known as Kamalpur railway station. Built in the style of a pavilion, with high, segmented domes having a touch of Islamic architecture, the station as a whole is quite modern and spacious. It has some eight or nine terminal platforms, but only one through track, which is meter-gauge in these parts. Train services too seem to be rather nominal at the moment—despite claims to the contrary by the Govern-

ment—because of an admitted acute shortage of
rolling stock and fuel.

Conditions at an inter-city bus stand nearby
are similar. From here Japanese mini-buses appear
to be departing for various destinations. But out
of fifty or so vehicles parked in the enclosure, only
ten seem to be fit for service. As a result, indescrib-
able over-loading is the norm and, as reported by
local newspapers, major disasters on the way are
an everyday occurrence. However, for the city's
internal service, some brand new Tata-Mercedes
buses, supplied by India, are now on the road, and
these are doing a fine job. They are not only well-
designed and good to look at but also strongly built.
Yet the riff-raff of the city can be overheard making
even these buses a target of ridicule for the only
reason that they are Indian-made.

In the centre of the area lies the commercial
complex, of which we have already spoken. Most
of the bigger companies, the banks, and many
Government departments have their offices here.
At its southern end, enclosed by a wall, is what was
formerly the Government House, now called Banga
Bhawan, being the residence of the President. It
is a magnificent, sprawling white mansion dating
from British times. You are allowed to look at it
only from the outside. Old Dacca begins from
here, and extends for about three miles along the
Buri Ganga river, flowing a little further south
from this place. One is reminded, on seeing the
imperial building, that during the December war the
IAF scored a direct hit on it, which event finally
persuaded the last Pakistani Governor, Dr. Malik,

to tender his resignation. The old man is now serving his life sentence.

Facing Banga Bhawan and adjacent to the entire Commercial Area is a vast rectangular complex of busy streets and crowded bazars, known collectively as Gulistan. It comprises a beautiful park decorated with fountains, an open space called Paltan Maidan and a seemingly incomplete stadium. Under the stadium, on the outer side, runs a circular market, which, along with the Maidan with its inevitable meeting, makes for much crowding here throughout the day. Finally, somewhat hidden by the stadium is that most famous building of Dacca which may well be called 'the symbol of this city'. Known as Masjid Baitul-Mukarram, it is a mosque of a new design or rather after the design of the Kaba in Mecca, but of far larger dimensions. On a raised plinth of wide stairs stands the gigantic central cube, as tall as an eight-storey building, with two well-proportioned wings perforated with open, arched windows, extending on either side. A large number of stalls and some markets are located near and under the mosque, giving it a hectic commercial air rather than a serene religious aura. The whole complex certainly serves as a fitting memorial to 24 years of Pakistani rule over this land.

A stone's throw from the Mosque stands the eight-storey building of the Bangladesh Secretariat. Further west, girded by a near-circular road, is that vast stretch of green which has come to acquire an unparalleled place in the history of Bangladesh's freedom struggle. It is the famous Race Course or Ramna

Maidan, now called Suhrawardy Uddyan. It was
from here that Sheikh Mujib announced the launch-
ing of Bangladesh's struggle for freedom on March
7, 1971. (Actually, on that date, he announced a
7-point compromise formula.) It was again here that
General Niazi signed the instrument of surrender
before General Arora on December 16, 1971.

At the southern fringe of the Maidan are the
present Supreme Court buildings, with the tombs
of Fazal-ul-Haq and Suhrawardy nearby, and on
the northern side stands the now-famous boat-dais,
named 'Indira Munch' in honour of Prime Minister
Indira Gandhi, who delivered her first address to
the people of Bangladesh on March 17, 1972 from
here. This entire, somewhat oval, vast expanse
of green, by its dimensions and the use to which
it is put now, brings to mind the Ram Lila ground
of Delhi with its own princely-looking, permanent
dais, though the shape and environment of the two
are entirely different.

To the south of the Maidan stretches the University area, and on the north are the lush green Ramna
Park with its enchanting serpentine lake, and the
Bangladesh Radio building, the latter seems rather
dwarfed by the towering Hotel Inter-Continental
nearby. The Hotel was made famous during the war
by the establishment there of an International Neutral
Zone and the stationing of an Indian tank in front of
it after victory. On the far side of the Park is another
green and well-shaded Civil Lines-like area, criss-
crossed by well-paved, clean roads, where the Prime
Minister's official residence, Gono Bhawan, and the
residences of most of the other Ministers and high

officials are situated. From the crossing in front of
the famous hotel runs a trunk road north to
Tejgaon Airport, and beyond to Mymensingh and
north Bangladesh.

The other half of new Dacca stretches further
west to the affluent residential locality of Dhanmandi (where most of the Embassies are) and, towards the north, to the new Government complex
of Sher-e-Bangal Nagar, which Ayub intended to
be the second capital, and beyond to the former
Bihari colonies of Mohammedpur and Mirpur.

Thus, within less than two hours, one can cover
the entire central part of new Dacca by just walking
around. No distance appears to be more than a
mile or so, and most of the important buildings
seem to be curiously grouped together within a
limited area, so much so that one can often see the
tops of all of them from many points in the city.
There is no question thus of anyone losing his way
here; even if one is lost, one can always come back
to the starting point by just keeping any one of the
familiar tops in view. Indeed, to a Delhi-wallah, the
maze of the city appears to be a child's play.

But this very concentration of the buildings
has given rise to a serious defect in that none of
them now seems to belong where it stands. In
fact, except for the Supreme Court buildings, not
a single structure in this entire area appears to be
in its proper place. Just think of the most magnificent mosque in the country's capital being over-
shadowed by a monstrous stadium!

Apart from this relative mislocation of buildings,
the other thing that a visitor feels while walking

in the streets relates to the physical make-up and behaviour of the passers-by. The normal male clothing here is the lungi and vest or shirt, kurta-pyjama, and pants-bushshirt. Similar clothing can be seen in many places in India too, especially around the industrial belt of Calcutta. Yet the people here look quite different; their demeanour is diffe. rent. For one thing, they generally seem to wear a somewhat dazed and bewildered expression ; they look as if they are not in contact, as if they have lost some valuable possession.

One also gets the feeling that most of the people here are perhaps from the lower strata of society, the so-called great proletariat; or perhaps they are the simple folk, the unsophisticated villagers. And the new-comer soon finds himself wondering as to what has become of the educated and respectable gentry, those well-dressed people known in Bengali as 'the bhadraloks'. Where are 'the bhadraloks'?

Furthermore, the streets are also totally devoid of that most precious thing in life—women and children. They are hardly noticeable. Their absence certainly cuts out all colour and laughter from the scene. And this entire arid, uninspiring situation in its cumulative effect soon becomes a source of great disappointment, irritation and boredom; or, worse still, you become gloomy and pessimistic about your own prospects for no reason whatsoever. All cheerfulness departs from your heart as you walk through the streets of present-day Dacca.

What is still more baffling and inexplicable is the nature of the response you get from people in the streets to genuine enquiries. As you stop or accost someone and enquire about the way or the place, etc., he just stares at you with a visible contraction of all his muscles. Only on repeating and further clarifying your query, would you be able to make him mumble something, which may not still be of any help to you. Something of the same kind is experienced at places, where you have to tap at some door to make enquiries about some tenant living there. The person opening the door would likewise just stare at you for some time, and only after much persuasion and show of politeness would you be able to elicit any helpful reply from him. What is all this?

During my stay in Dacca, I had long discussions with various educated persons on this entire situation, and the gist of those talks can be set down here somewhat as follows :

1. Civic confidence is not yet fully restored, not even in Dacca; so the gentry, and women and children, in particular, do not come out much in the streets.

2. The reason for the feeling of unpleasantness and depression is simply the sight of mostly hungry-looking, haggard and half-clad people in the streets.

3. The people generally are so engrossed in their own problems of livelihood that they have neither the time nor the mood to welcome stupid questions from strangers.

4. People here probably find it difficult to follow the Calcutta accent; so, they are naturally slowed down in showing their reactions.

5.   Or else, the people here are so dull-headed
     that unless a question is repeated several
     times, they just cannot form any idea of it.
     (The last "explanation" was used only as
     a provocation.)

On this rather frank but cleverly-worded analysis
of the observations made, the persons I talked to
made their comments. Of them, what a Bangladeshi journalist, a young publicity officer, and a
former MCA said on different occasions seems to be
pertinent enough to be quoted here. Since, however, all three agreed on most of the vital points,
their comments would perhaps be best represented
by consolidating them into a statement. So, here
is the average Bangladeshi intellect speaking to the
average Indian intellect; that it offers a key to an
understanding of present-day Bangladesh is, of
course, beyond doubt :

What you call 'the element of delayed reaction'
in the character of our people may well be caused,
in individual cases, by any of the three circumstances
that you have mentioned, namely, that they may
be pre-occupied, that they may really find it difficult
to follow your accent, or that some of them may
really be dull-headed. But, according to our lights,
the reason nearest the truth is something else:
it is our history of the past 15 years or so, particularly the history of the final year before liberation. During this period, what our people have
gone through has never been seen by the eyes of
any people. The wide-eyed, tongue-tied man who
just stares at you on being accosted and questioned
is simply giving you a glimpse of those days of

horror when his very life depended on the kind of reply he would give to an armed soldier or Razakar. Obviously, he could not take chances with such a matter of life and death to him by reacting in haste and without due deliberation; after all his very survival was at stake. So, by constant practice, or rather forced practice, actually spread over a much longer period than the nine months of terror the world has heard of, he has come to acquire this peculiar but very useful habit of looking long before he leaps. The habit is so old and so deeply-rooted that a mere year of freedom and fundamental rights has not been long enough, obviously, to erase it completely.

You, friends from across the border, who have breathed the free and democratic air of India, can scarcely imagine what it is like to live under naked military rule year after year, and how the constant fear of the fixed bayonet can degrade and distort the character of an ordinary working man. Believe us that no written record, however comprehensive, of the atrocities committed by Yahya's hordes on our people can reveal as much as those dark lines of terror that appear on the face of a common man here when he is suddenly confronted and questioned by a light-complexioned and well-dressed person like you.

All that can be added to this explanation is that it was not in their closing days only that the Pakistani rulers brought our common people to this mental pass—which has caused you some inconvenience. They had, in fact, throughout their rule given them such lessons also as worked to retard the normal growth of their intelligence. Pakistani politics of a religious state has instilled the most fantastic ideas in the minds of our people, the evil effects of which are still operating. But, on the other hand, the direct experience of concrete realities, such as the coming forward of your country to our aid, the laying down of their lives for us on our soil by your soldiers, etc., has clearly demonstrated the falsity of some of our people's most cherished convictions. This cannot but cause them a lot of confusion and bewilderment, and this confusion is also one of the reasons for their present seemingly abnormal behaviour.

So far as your first observation is concerned— that you see few 'bhadraloks' in the streets—there is, no doubt, some truth in it. We do not deny either that women and children are not coming out yet in sufficient numbers to make an impact on you; it was not like this in the past, though. This particular situation has its origin in the unleashing of Pak military terror in early 1971, and it has not yet been completely normalised. But as for 'gentry' —what you call the 'upper class,' that is, 'posh people' in your country—such people no longer exist here. Such a class in our country was composed mainly of the Pakistanis, who have either fled the land or are at present held jointly by us as POWs. Amongst us Bangladeshis, so to say, the so-called rich and mighty are too few to be counted as a class. Yet the real reason for your observation is altogether different, and it is very simple. It is nothing more than the physical make-up of our people and the present standards of their clothing.

Now, the facts are that even ordinary cotton fabrics are in acute short supply here at the moment; as for the finer varieties, their import is totally banned. So, the first point is that our people have to make do with old clothes for the time being. Then, during these months, the weather too, with its high humidity ratio, becomes a factor contributing to shabbiness. To these economic and climatic reasons has now been added another factor. It is the revolutionary struggle of the recent past which has certainly had a decisive influence in downgrading appearances. Common endeavour has definitely brought about a visible shift in social norms and standards, with the result that few people amongst us today seem to bother much about what they are wearing. Finally, we have this special apparel, lungi, which is a sort of formal clothing here for all people ; it is so from this country right down to Indonesia. But amongst you Indians, we suppose, it is generally not used by educated people outside the precincts of their houses. So, what it boils down to is this that amongst the same shabby-looking and scantily-dressed people that you see in the streets, our educated middle class is also present. But since your eyes are accustomed to the human environment of cities like Delhi and Calcutta, you feel you do not see them.

As for your sense of disappointment and depression, we think it is partly due to the present bad shape of our economy, of which you can see ample signs all around. But poverty, even dire poverty, is no new thing either to you or to us. Therefore, we assume that the main reason is again the same which we ventured to suggest in connection with your first observation, that is, you are a person from Delhi and Calcutta, acclimatised to the atmosphere there. And here, unfortunately for the time being, you do not see those 'embodiments of charm and elegance' which no important and modern city in the world today can afford to do without! So, that's the reason for your feeling of depression! However, we invite you to visit us again in another few years' time, and we can assure you that on the next occasion you will not have to complain that the air in Dacca hasn't got that magic touch which is so pronounced in Delhi and Calcutta !

On return to Delhi later, it didn't take the sensitive writer long to be convinced of the correctness of the insight of those Bangladeshi friends !

CHAPTER 3

Muscles of Law and Laws of Muscle !

SECURITY AT the Bangladesh Secretariat in Dacca is such that all you have to do to jump it, is to take a large-sized brief-case in your hand and, keeping your eyes straight and neck stiff, just walk past the sentries at the gate with an air of supreme indifference. None can dare stop you. Once in, you can loiter about the corridors at will, step into any office you like, and generally have a good time—which, incidentally, is what most of the other people there will be doing. No one will so much as tap you on the shoulder to find out the nature of your business, for, indeed, there is not much for anyone to do here.

But, if out of a sense of respect for regulations, you think it proper to get a visitor's pass made out for you at the outer reception, you will most probably be told that you have come at the wrong hour, that only between 12 noon and 1 p.m. can visitors be allowed in, and, further, that your name must also appear on the day's list of visitors. Since, however, your name cannot possibly be there, at least not on the first day, because you cannot possibly know which officer is to be approached for sorting out your problem, you will have to wait for another occasion. You may even decide to write off the whole idea of having anything further to do with this Government. Having been in and out of the Secretariat building almost daily for about a week by the direct method, this writer did exactly that after bumping against regulations : I simply struck off the ill-placed building from the list of my daily haunts.

However, on the first day, entry was gained by the aforesaid direct method, and after a day-long effort and much ado, some kind of an arrangement for the writer's temporary stay in Dacca was eventually struck up. It so happened that the nation's Parliament was not in session just then ; so the MP Hostel behind the provisional Parliament House (Jatiya Parishad) near the Airport lay almost vacant. A public relations campaign to secure a room in that hostel was therefore launched by two of us ; that is, the writer and the Times of India's Special Correspondent in Dacca, Mr. Kirit Bhaumik, for whom I had letter of introduction from Mr. Girilal Jain, the Resident Editor in Delhi. The expedition was crowned with success, for which the credit goes to the Principal Information Officer of Bangladesh, Mr. Inam-ul-Haq, and, of course, to Mr. Bhaumik, without whose dedicated interest and able support nothing could have been achieved. I wish to record here my deep sense of gratitude to all these three gentlemen.

The same evening as I was coming out of Mr. Haq's office with his letter of recommendation, a loquacious assistant who had filled my hours of waiting with his revolutionary talk on India-Bangladesh friendship, followed me quietly to the courtyard, and taking me aside whispered in my ear: "Dada, got any Indian currency...how about 50 per cent premium . . . ?"

Cutting him short, I said, "No currency, brother, and no brains either. So, you see . . ."

But a little later as I walked down the street, I became curious as to whether that small functionary was only on the look-out for an extra bit on the side, or was tactfully checking on 'a foreigner' on behalf of some intelligence set-up. He didn't look like a man from the Secret Police or the Customs, for it is really not difficult to recognise the hardened professionals in these lines. In any case, my final judgement was that the man had acted in his individual capacity.

On this question of check-up or surveillance, it would not be out of place to mention here that during my entire 16-day stay in Bangladesh, I did not notice any such thing at all. It may sound rather strange to say that surveillance was not 'noticed'. But the explanation is that this writer, an 'old sinner', is so used to getting wise to surveillance that one of his special pleasures has always been to give the benefit of his direct company to the otherwise bewildered and harassed agent keeping the futile watch on him.

Mr. Bhaumik had taken me to a joint of Indian correspondents in Dacca late that very evening. Most of these pressmen in Dacca are, of course, Bengalis, representing the national papers of Delhi

and Calcutta. During the professional tete-a-tete
that inevitably followed, only two points of personal
interest to me emerged. One was that a journey
to Chittagong and then to north Bangladesh by the
land route was not going to be a feasible proposition
for a weakling like me; if at all travel was necessary,
air was the only means. That, financially speaking,
put an end to all the intricate scheming gone into
by the family back home to regain its rights in
Bangladesh. Correspondence with the local authorities was now the only means left. The second
point concerned the idea of surveillance.

It turned out that these Indian correspondents
in Dacca laboured under the delusion that they were
being kept under strict surveillance by the Bangladesh Government. With only three days' experience
in Dacca, I thought it fit to keep my mouth shut
on that occasion. But, later on, I could not restrain
myself from telling one or two of these co-
professionals plainly that far from maintaining a
watch on the Indians here, the Government of
Bangladesh was perhaps not even aware how many
of our own agents, some of them very highly-placed,
were keeping a constant watch on it !

Flippancy apart, the real reason for this persistent idea of persecution harboured by our newsmen
in Dacca—it comes naturally to all true-bred
Bengalis in an alien setting—is nothing more than
the irregularity in their mail. Like the Railways
and the bus services in Bangladesh today, the Posts
and Telegraphs are also in a very bad shape, due
mainly to the elimination of most of the older and
experienced Bihari staff and their replacement with

Bangladeshi novices. Mail in Bangladesh today is not only irregular, it is also unreliable ; much of it simply disappears between the letter-box and the addressees. It is this circumstance which gives our newsmen the idea that their correspondence is subject to secret censorship. But where mail is secretly censored, it should never disappear, or else there is no point in such censorship, for the correspondents could at once switch over to other means—the diplomatic bag is always there for anything really important. (Don't tell me that India's diplomatic bag in Dacca cannot be used for purposes other than diplomatic !) So, what seems to be happening is nothing more than plain, petty larceny. Dishonest postmen, and new hands not attuned to the ethics of Posts, seem to be responsible for it.

Even ordinary administration of a working standard has not yet been re-established in Bangladesh, what to speak of such sophisticated set-ups as a secret service or Intelligence network. In the capital itself, the streets become deserted as dusk falls, and goondas and gangsters begin to rule the roost. The countryside is still left to the depradations of criminals. Murders, said to be political, are the order of the day, and day-light robberies are a common occurrence. The most unfortunate aspect of the situation is that groups of erstwhile patriots who, in the name of the much-eulogised 'Mukti Bahini', used to throw bombs on Pak Army installations, have now engaged themselves in organised dacoities in the countryside. Some of these boys are from good families and are

highly educated. But when asked by those who
wish them well why they have taken to such evil
ways, their pet reply is : 'Because the ways of virtue
are closed on us.' Really, what kind of a national
revolution is this which, instead of creating a new
spirit and passion for reconstruction, has driven
these brave young men into such blind alleys of self-
pity and self-destruction.

The main reason for the present weakness and
waywardness of the administration in Bangladesh
is the immaturity and inexperience of most of the
new personnel recruited after liberation, particularly
the Police force, most of the older one having been
exterminated by the Pakistani Army. In the past,
almost all top positions in the hierarchy were held
by Pakistani officers—which circumstance was itself one of the causes of the Independence movement
here. With the advent of freedom, all those experienced officers just disappeared, and their positions were taken up by Bangladeshi juniors and
new recruits, the latter inducted not on merits but
for political considerations. These sons and nephews
of political upstarts have neither any experience
of running an organised administration, nor are
they honest and principled enough to resist the
pull of personal greed or undue political pressure.
As a result, there is a general collapse of the entire
administrative apparatus.

Then, there is the additional difficulty of orientation. Even the older personnel, who have worked
only in subordinate positions under a provincial
government, have no conception of how a central,
national government is run. Whatever initiative

or decision-making abilities they ever possessed were stamped out under the jackboot of the military. Thus, the habit of looking up to higher authority is so ingrained in them that the biggest joke now going its rounds in the Bangladesh Secretariat is related somewhat as follows :

Officer: Hey ! Send this wireless to Islamabad for instructions !

Operator: Sorry, Sir, no contact.

Officer: All right. Send the damn thing to Delhi.

No doubt, this bad joke has been invented by someone wanting to satirize on the independence of Bangladesh. But the fact remains that most of the officers in the new 'Central' departments really do not know what their respective areas of functioning are, no rational distribution and organisation of work having yet been undertaken. The result is that 90 p.c. of the staff in these departments just while away their hours in idle gossip. Sheikh Mujib himself has admitted more than once that the Dacca Secretariat was nothing more than a municipal office; so the people who work here have minds fit only for municipal affairs.

The fundamental difficulty is that most of Bangladesh's top-level, experienced central officers are at present stranded in Pakistan. So, when Sheikh Mujib insists on the early repatriation of his 'four lakh compatriots' from Pakistan, he is not motivated only by 'brotherly love' or humanitarian considerations for the plight of his countrymen but also by his dire need to get back his experienced

officers to help him set up a strong administration.
Besides, he is particularly desirous of getting back
the 28,000 Bangladeshi soldiers, who formed part
of the regular Pak army, but who are now confined
to concentration camps on the N.W. Frontier.

In Bangladesh itself, the Bangla regiments, by
raising the banner of revolt against their then
masters and siding with the Awami League's freedom struggle, might have done a great patriotic
and self-sacrificing act. Yet there is no denying
that, in principle, they did violate their oath of
allegiance, and, to that extent, they were contami-
nated with politics. And this aspect of a professional
military force is something which no parliamentary
democracy can ever view with equanimity. In
fact, in this matter, the present Bangladesh army,
which is composed mostly of these 'rebel' regiments,
has come to acquire a position very similar to that
of the Indian National Army on the eve of Indian
Independence. And everyone knows what treatment was meted out to that patriotic force by the
Congress government of India after it took over.
So, very naturally and understandably, Sheikh
Mujib too desires that his top officers, and the
soldiers in particular, should return home as early
as possible, so that by screening and selecting from
them, he could build an efficient administration as
well as a 'clean', non-political army and police for
his state.

Leaving aside the question of the all-too-evident
weakness of the Administration, no observer can,
however, deny that freedom of politics as such,
including even that of the communal variety, is

rather too extensive in Bangladesh at the moment. In a sense, the people have got what amounts to a total licence in the name of political freedom. The leadership being immature, the result inevitably is that freedom is being universally misused by all political parties, more so by the ruling party, for it has the power both of larger numbers and more funds at its disposal.

Meetings and processions of all kinds and provocative slogan-mongering are the order of the day, but even direct political highhandedness and gangsterism are no less in evidence. Since all legal parties are ostensibly agreed on the basic question of an independent Bangladesh, the easiest way to strip anyone of his surplus cash is to label him 'an anti-Bangladesh, Pakistani agent,' and then to abduct him straightaway and release him only after extorting a heavy ransom. This operation, in local political parlance, is called 'hijacking', and any citizen can be made a victim of it if only he is known to possess some hard cash or other valuables. In fact, the main reason why the gentry, and women and children are not seen much in the streets is the widespread fear of this kind of political banditry.

No doubt, this entire situation is partly due to the present weakness of the law-enforcing machinery ; but another reason for it is the absence of any organised opposition in the country. This may sound rather paradoxical. But the fact is that in Bangladesh today, opposition is confined only to the street or the maidan ; in the national Parliament and the Establishment, it has virtually no place. At the top, only the Awami League counts. The

entire elite of the country—the owners of intellectul
and material resources who, under any dispensation,
must constitute the ruling class—are solidly behind
the Awami League government. Therefore, even
if weak in structure, the Government can well
afford to give the so-called opposition a long rope.
But this very leniency on its part leads to a much
exaggerated impression of the opposition to itself;
the intensity of opposition appears to be far greater
than what it really is. Since the frustrated leaders
of the so-called opposition have no access to the
loaves and fishes of office, they must make up for
their loss of comfort by indulging in inflammatory
rhetoric and provocative slogan-mongering on the
Maidan. Thereupon, the lathi-wielding muscle-men
of the powerful Awami League make their appearance on the scene, and there are pitched battles
to settle issues that cannot be thrashed out on a
democratic forum, because there is none. It is
thus that party politics in Bangladesh has assumed
its present war-like dimensions. If the so-called
opposition had also some seats in Parliament, and
were given some representation on its committees,
commissions, and delegations, neither the use of
political freedom would have assumed such irres-
ponsible overtones, nor the Government would
have been faced with the kind of malicious criticism
it has been putting up with since the day of its
inception.

An important feature of party politics in Bangladesh today is the numerous fronts which almost
every political party has built up around itself.
Moreover, the 'dadas' who control these fronts have
their own private, paid 'bahinis'—the red caps and

all that—who are ever ready to break other people's heads.

The ruling Awami League has its Chhatra League, the Yuva League, the Shramik League, the Krishak League and what not. Similarly, the NAP (Muzaffar) has its Chhatra Union and other fronts, and the NAP (Bhashani) has its Biplabi Chhatra Union and peasant fronts. There are some other student organisations, such as the Bangla Chhatra Union, Purba Bangla Chhatra Union and clandestine 'Muslim Chhatra Union', etc. The other two noteworthy parties are the Bangladesh Communist Party of the veteran leader Comrade Moni Singh, and the National Socialist Party (Jatiya Samajtantrik Dal) of Mukti Bahini's Major Jalil, who is said to have been dismissed from the Army, because of his extremist views. Among these two, the former has little influence on national politics here, while the latter party, by its organisation and leadership. seems to be a fascist gang-up, presumably financed from abroad. Even its name is reminiscent of Hitler, and its methods of work and propaganda are very similar to those adopted by the Nazi party in Germany. Only the Feuhrer is still to emerge.

Student organisations still exercise a tremendous influence on Bangladesh politics. Previously, all these splinter groups worked under the banner of East Pakistan Chhatra League. That body had thrown up four leaders of some eminence. They were Abdur Rab, Shahjehan Seraj, Nur Alam Siddiqui, and Abdul Quddoos Makhan. Immediately after liberation, these four young men were said to have exercised such influence on the Prime Minister that they came to be referred to as 'the Four Khalifas of Mujib.' Later on, they parted ways on the question of collaboration with the Awami League. Rab and Seraj, calling for what they termed as 'scientific socialism', joined hands with the mysterious Major Jalil to form the JSD, while the other two, with the main body of the Chhatra League, supported the Sheikh and his government. As a reward, one of them, Makhan, is now an MP.

It is clear from the above that the student organisations of Bangladesh are not just University or college unions or bodies concerned mainly with education; they are in fact full-fledged political parties. And like the electioneering parties with which they are associated, they too have their own district, town, and ward branches. These branches are so numerous and widespread that at places one can see three or four branch offices with the same name. It is really an extraordinary situation.

On enquiry, it turned out that the real branch office is perhaps only one of them or none at all, and that, as a rule, these are only abandoned houses or such houses from which the inmates have been thrown out and the premises occupied illegally. And to give such forcible occupation a sort of formal sanction, a sign-board bearing the name of some legal party or union has been hung up on the premises. In plain words, any 'dada', who along with his gang has occupied a vacant house, has put up the name of his party or union on it instead of his own, and having thus given it the legal air of a formal allotment, has started living there like a landlord, letting out the house to needy tenants. Obviously, such expropriation could be committed and was committed mostly in the name of the ruling party, but to prevent other political parties from raising much noise over it, some houses have also been left for them to capture. Thus, in Bangladesh today, two trades seem to be very much on the ascending curve: one is that of painting sign-boards (Every third person in Bangladesh seems to need a new sign-board !), and the other is the unauthorised occupation of houses and illegal land-lordism.

The worst thing that has happened in this direction is that the youth and the student community have fallen a prey to the lure of money. The youth the world over have of late acquired many defects from the point of view of the old: they care little for old-style discipline, they seem to demand sexual permissiveness, and they exhibit a certain proclivity to violence and destructiveness. But love of money and worship of Mammon are certainly not among their faults. It was left for the youth of Bangladesh to earn the unique distinction of regarding money as the sole purpose of politics. And in this, they seem to have gone far ahead of their own and our politicians. To what extent the rot has set in can be imagined by the fact that when looted property is recovered from the sons and nephews of Sheikh Mujib himself, the moralists are told off by the disarming comment: "What harm is done if those who gave their blood for the country's freedom enjoyed for some time the use of certain things they really needed ?"

When the aggrieved persons go to Sheikh Saheb with complaints, he at once assumes the posture of a saint, raises both his hands towards heaven, and, shedding hot, fresh tears of remorse, laments in classical Bengali: "Allah ! take me away from this wretched world of evil and sin; I have no desire to live any more ! What is all this happening around me ?"—and at that the matter ends. Many people say that the Sheikh's real guru is no longer Suhrawardy; it is Jawaharlal Nehru !

CHAPTER 4

The Four Pillars of 'Mujibism'—
A Marxist View

THE FOUR ideals of Nationalism, Democracy, Socialism, and Secularism, enshrined in its Constitution by the People's Republic of Bangladesh, are also known collectively as 'Mujibism'. How Sheikh Mujib himself interprets and elucidates these concepts is seen from his innumerable speeches and statements which have found an equally ready outlet in the Indian press. Therefore, no recapitulation of his utterances seems to be necessary here. What our people would perhaps be more interested to know is how some of the other parties, which also claim to endorse and support these principles, look at them. So, to find that out, I made my first call in Dacca on the leader of the so-called pro-Moscow National Awami Party, Professor Muzaffar Ahmed.

There was no particular reason for this preference, except that it was the sign-board of the Central Headquarters of *his* party that caught my eye every time I came out of the Secretariat.

Therefore, as a matter of convenience, I thought it best to commence my research with the Professor.

According to the life-sketch given to me by his office, Professor Ahmed was born in 1922 in a middle-class family of a village called 'Allahabad' in the district of Comilla. His father was the late Alhaj Qayamuddin Bhuinya. He graduated from Calcutta University in 1944 and got his M.A. degree in Economics in 1946 from Dacca University. Thereafter, he taught economics in different Government colleges and Dacca University till 1954, when, as a candidate of Suhrawardy's United Front in the first General Election in East Pakistan, he trounced the Muslim League Minister, Mufeezuddin, from his home constituency by a thumping majority.

The most notable feature of his political career seems to have been his knack for going underground whenever things became hot for him. For instance, after the imposition of martial law under Ayub Khan, in 1958, he remained underground for full eight years, till 1966. Again, after the Pak military crackdown in early 1971, he disappeared, and organised the resistance movement in the country-side, while also serving on the Consultative Council attached to the Provisional Government of Bangladesh at Mujib Nagar. After liberation, in 1972, he was re-elected President of his party—which post he still holds.

In formal interview, Professor Ahmed appears to be an extremely serious and reserved person. Quite oblivious of the presence of his interviewer, he goes on staring steadily into vacuum, as if his entire attention were concentrated on some matter of high importance. From this excessive aloofness, preoccupation, and lack of warmth which he makes no effort to conceal, he can be easily mistaken for a committed Marxist, even a fanatical communist. But perhaps the many signs of detachment, even of melancholia, that can be detected in his personality are a product of his recurring underground life and secret revolutionary activities over long periods. In responding to questions, however, he is very precise in his language and logical in argument, though the content of what he says does at times gives the impression of an extraordinary approach.

Having grasped the nature and direction of my inquiry, he started reeling off a series of well-constructed English sentences:

"Nationalism has certain very definite connotations", he began, taking up the first principle of Mujibism. "But the kind of nationalism we have here is still an open question. I find in it three contradictions and the same number of conformities. First, the majority here, that is those who are so called on the basis of religion, have been taught during the past 25-30 years that as Muslims they are a nation. Without a doubt, it is an entirely false and absurd notion; there is no such thing as a 'Muslim nation' anywhere in the world today. Of course, there are many nations that are Muslim, but Muslims as such do not constitute a nation. However, as you know, Pakistan, of which our Bangladesh was a part, was established on the basis of what was known as the 'two-nation theory', that is, the hypothesis that all the Muslims of the sub-continent, or at least of those parts which

could become Pakistan, were a nation, while the
Hindus of the sub-continent constituted the other
nation. Thus, the first definition of nationalism
here is this Islamic nationalism. And, however
false and hypothetical, it is still a living and active
force, continuing to have its impact on the minds
of many of our people. This is the first contradiction in our concept of Bangladeshi nationalism.

The second contradiction arises out of our concept of Bengali nationalism, which is based on
language and culture. But then, scientifically
speaking, it would mean that all the Bengali-speaking
people, irrespective of their place of residence or
the religion they follow, are one nation. That is
to say, the people of your Bengal and the other
Bengali-speaking people of the neighbouring Indian
states are all part of this Bengali nation together with
us. But, evidently, that is not the concrete situation;
the Bengali-speaking people are, in practice, divided
into more than one nation and sub-nationalities.
Thus, according to the practical situation as it
obtains, only the people of our Bangladesh are a
nation, irrespective of any distinction of caste and
creed, while the other Bengalis, also irrespective of
any distinction of caste and creed, form part of your
great Indian nation.

The third contradiction, which, in effect, resolves
the problem, is the separate existence of our Bangladesh as an independent state. Behind it lie not
only the language and culture of our people but
also their special experience of 24 years of living in
Pakistan and the history of their struggle for freedom from Pakistani domination—an experience

and history in which the Bengali-speaking people of India have had no direct share. From this standpoint, the separate existence of Bangladesh as a state is quite reasonable and justified, though not as a separate nation".

Q: Please clarify.

A: You see, while it is possible to prove scientifically that all Bengalis are one nation, yet, even as one nation, they can have two or more separate independent states; and all those states would be scientifically justified.

Q: You mean like the two states of the German nation, or the 16 states of the Arabs ?

A: Yes, something like that, though the position of the Bengalis is quite different from these other nations ; the Bengalis as such have so far only one independent state !

Q: But Sheikh Mujib says that the Bangladeshis are a nation by themselves because they have gone through the specific experience of a struggle for freedom within the context of Pakistan. And it is this experience and the struggle which give them their sense of distinct nationhood ?

A: Correct. But when our present rulers evoke this specific experience of an exclusive struggle for freedom in justification of the separate nationhood of the Bangladeshis, their assertions are not motivated by genuine regard for truth; they talk like this merely to assuage *your* misgivings about Greater Bengal, that is, to prevent the slogan of United Bengal from being raised on both sides of the border,

Q: Should I take it then that your party supports the idea of a Greater Bengal ?

A: My party thinks that, scientifically speaking, a Bengali nation should include all people who speak Bengali, irrespective of their experiences of life. But since, by a quirk of fate, this Bangladesh of ours has come into existence as an independent state, while you, the other Bengalis, are a member of the great Indian Union out of your own free choice, we regard the two states; that is, independent Bangladesh and the autonomous state of Bengal within India, as scientifically correct and justified, though we do not make any distinction between the Bengalis on either side of the border. For myself, I feel as much at home in Calcutta as here, and I presume you too in Dacca must be having the same feeling of being at home.

Q: In this matter, Sir, my own opinion is still reserved. Let us pass on to the second pillar, which is Democracy.

A: Yes, but unless you define what kind of democracy is intended—parliamentary, presidential, socialistic, populist, or just basic—it takes you nowhere to say that you want democracy. Nevertheless, it is true that our people had some experience of a certain kind of democracy in the past, and that was the British model of parliamentary democracy. Naturally, therefore, after Independence, our rulers made a show of adopting it. But I feel that even this kind of democracy is in great danger of going down here, because of the attitude of our ruling party, which seems to believe not in democracy but in one-party rule. In plain words, the ruling

Awami League here is aiming at establishing a one-party state.

Now, if you believe in such a system, you should be honest enough to declare that you do not believe in parliamentary democracy, that you believe in the fascist dictum of 'one state, one party, one leader', etc. But if you say that you believe in parliamentary democracy, then you must also believe in at least a two-party system. Unfortunately, I do not see any such honesty on the part of the ruling party here. Sheikh Saheb does not in the least seem to be inclined to grant the status of Opposition to any party; he has not allowed any of our candidates to be elected to Parliament. I am, therefore, not very optimistic about the success of parliamentary democracy in this country.

Q: But why and how can you expect Sheikh Mujib to allow any of your candidates to be elected ?

A : Correct. But we must not forget that democracy in this country is still a very tender plant. If, therefore, some special care is not taken right from the beginning, some healthy conventions are not initiated, democracy may not grow here at all.

Take the example of your Jawaharlal Nehru. He certainly believed in parliamentary democracy. And so, he used to exercise his own influence to get a fair number of opposition candidates elected to Parliament, and he saw to it that they were given due recognition as an opposition. In this way, he always tried to place at least two alternatives before the people, so that they could compare and choose

what they thought was better for them. I dare
say the credit for whatever success parliamentary
democracy has achieved in your country goes
entirely to that great man.

Q: Now, what about secularism in Bangladesh?
It must be confusing to many of your people, isn't
it?

A: Everyone knows that secularism cannot
become a reality unless socialism is first established.
So long as the system of capitalistic exploitation
goes on, the owners of wealth and power must use
one section against another, one community against
another, and so on, because it cannot be in their
interest to allow the poor and labouring classes to
discover their true identity and forge a common
front against them. All these Hindu-Muslim, Bengali-
Bihari, and district versus district conflicts are the
creations of the capitalist class. Therefore, I have
no doubt that so long as capitalism is not done
away with, secularism will remain only an empty
word.

Q: How is your Hindu minority going to fare
then in secular Bangladesh ?

A: The Hindus in this country have no longer
any vested interest; they do not compete with or
confront the majority community in any field of
activity. They are the working people, making
their living mostly as labourers, cultivators, and
petty shop-keepers. In fact, the reason why the
Pakistani type of aggressive communalism received
such a serious set-back here and our people were
able to resist Pakistani exploitation with such

resounding success, was that the Hindus in this
country were nowhere in the picture. Even now,
when communalism is still present amongst us and
raises its head every now and then, it is not because
of any conflict of interests between the majority
and the Hindu minority here. The real reason
lies in the conflict that exists between the business
interests of our incipient capitalist class and that of
yours; that is, the competition between our two
countries as two states—that is at the root of the
trouble. It is to gain their ends in this conflict that
our petty capitalists finance anti-Indian campaigns
here; they are spending a lot of money on this right
now, hiring all the old-timers on this single job.
The Government too is very much in it, for it
has to be, essentially, an agent of the capitalists.
But the trouble is that this anti-India feeling, which
they create mainly for business purposes, turns very
easily into an anti-Hindu one. For, in the minds
of our people, there is a direct link between India
and Hindu. That is the reason why when the
alleged smuggling of rice into India is talked about,
it takes no effort to convince our gullible people
that the Hindus are behind it, or that the Hindu
Food Minister is engaged in this traitorous activity.
Thus the main difficulty we face here in our fight
against communalism, is that no discussion about
India is possible without bringing in the poor local
Hindu, whose sole interest today is to be left alone.
And this confusion or involvement is what provides
the ground for communalism and anti-Hindu feeling
here.

Q: And socialism ?

A: As I have already said, the final remedy

for all the miseries of our people is the eradication
of capitalism and the establishment of full-fledged
socialism. So far, it has been adopted only as a
principle, or rather a claim has been made about
its adoption. Therefore, for the time being, there
is no question of its establishment or consummation.
The question merely is whether the path that has
been chosen will lead eventually to socialism or in
the opposite direction. In other words, the choice
at present is confined only to a suitable road to
socialism; the destination itself is still very, very
far off.

We have not forgotten how our people were
deceived in the past, how they were befooled and
beguiled in the name of Islam, of Islamic justice
and equality and all that. The result of that
continuous game of deception and falsehood has
been the unprecedented bloodshed, death and
destruction through which we have just passed.
But I am afraid the high-sounding slogans of
socialism that are now being raised may also turn
out to be as hollow as the Islamic ones. And,
then, nobody can say what the result would be.
I express my fears because I find that the personal
behaviour and style of living of most of our present
rulers have no relation whatever to the living conditions of the mass of our people. Even so, we are prepared to wait and see in what direction the socialistic
pretensions of our rulers take our country in the
coming years.

My party thinks that the various paper steps
taken so far in the name of socialism, namely, the
nationalisation of heavy industry, banks, etc.,

should be given a fair chance to materialise and fructify. There is no point, therefore, in casting doubts on the intentions of our rulers. Instead, we believe, pressure should be put on the Government to compel it to translate its professions into practice. The Government must be compelled by mass action to usher in socialism or face the prospect of being thrown out. If they fail, other parties must take over.

Q: Would your party then continue to co-operate with the Government in the building of socialism ?

A: Our co-operation will depend on the attitude of the Government. We believe in the unity of all progressive parties for the building of socialism, and my party will continue to extend full support to all progressive steps of the Government.

Q: Now, would you please say something about the future of your Bihari minority ?

A: Those among the Biharis who have opted for Pakistani citizenship are clearly Pakistan's responsibility, and Pakistan is duty bound to accept them. As for the rest, I think they will gradually adjust themselves to the conditions here. They are, no doubt, a linguistic minority. But their main problem today is really not language or culture, but rather of economic survival. Ways will, therefore, have to be found to rehabilitate them, that is, those who have chosen to stay on here, within our society. In any case, I believe it is a temporary problem.

It must, however, be made clear that national

minorities, whether they are religious or linguistic or of some other variety, must necessarily and for their own sake associate themselves with the larger interests of the people among whom they live. Only by discharging their national and social duties as citizens, can they hope to gain any rights. Or else in the present competitive, democratic world, no special privileges can accrue to any minority merely because it happens to be a minority.

Q: And, finally, how do you visualise the future of India-Bangladesh friendship ?

A: This question of friendly relations is not confined to India and Bangladesh alone, rather it is a question of India's relations with all its small neighbours. And, in this matter, it greatly pains me to say that despite being the biggest and the most powerful country in this region, India has not yet been able to establish its relations with its small neighbours on an even and sound basis. All the countries around it—Burma, Nepal, Sri Lanka, and even Bangladesh—are all the time apprehensive about their big brother's intentions. That is bad, and I think it is clearly India's responsibility to have these fears removed.

For us, here in Bangladesh, to believe in friendship with India is not merely an emotional necessity; in fact, our very existence and all our progressive policies depend on it. In plain words, without India-Bangladesh friendship, none of the four principles of our state policy can have a leg to stand upon. Especially for parties like mine, it is a question of life and death; without India's friendship, you see, my politics wouldn't just work here.

That is the reason why among all of Bangladesh's political parties, my party is most concerned and most determined to maintain and continually strengthen friendship with India.

As a matter of fact, I personally believe in the necessity of friendly unity of this entire sub-continent. For, frankly speaking, I do not see any way to end the miseries of the one-fifth of the human race inhabiting this region other than by unity and co-operation. In that sense, of course, you can say that I regard this sub-continent as one unit and its humanity as one people.

———

CHAPTER 5

'The Untold Story' by Manoranjan Dhar

VERY FEW people in India seem to remember that among the political parties of Bangladesh, there is one called the National Congress. Today, the full name of this party is Bangladesh Jatiya Congress. It is not the same Congress though, which was left in East Bengal after Partition as part of the Bengal branch of the then Indian National Congress. That old Congress had died with Partition itself, because most of its East Bengali leaders just crossed over to West Bengal after the vivisection, and one of them, Dr. Profulla Ghosh, was installed as Chief Minister of West Bengal as a sop to those East Bengali leaders.

Even so, quite a number of Congress members remained in the then Pakistan Constituent Assembly at Karachi and the East Bengal Assembly at Dacca, and these members assumed the role of the Opposition to the then ruling Muslim League. These Congressites in Pakistan later held a Convention at Dacca in August 1948, and resolved to form a new party under the name of 'Pakistan National

Congress'. But since conditions in West Pakistan
by then had taken a different turn, the new
Congress party soon came to be confined only to
East Pakistan. It functioned there till 1958 when
all parties were banned under Ayub's martial law.
The party was revived in 1962, but was again
suppressed in 1971.

One of the leading lights of this Congress has
been a lawyer from Mymensingh, named Manoranjan
Dhar. His name had often appeared on the political horizon even in erstwhile East Pakistan, both
as an Opposition leader and sometimes as a Minister.
Later, during the struggle for Bangladesh, he is
known to have collaborated closely with the Awami
League, working with its provisional government
at Mujibnagar. Now, in the present set-up of the
new Republic, he is naturally one of the top figures.
As the Minister of Law and Parliamentary Affairs
in the new Cabinet, he is one of Sheikh Mujib's most
trusted colleagues.

According to his official life-sketch, Shri Manoranjan Dhar was born on February 21, 1904 in a
village called Chatal in Mymensingh district. He
is a law graduate from Calcutta University, and
has been an eminent lawyer in the High Court of
erstwhile East Pakistan.

When still a boy of 13, he started taking part
in anti-British revolutionary activities as a member
of the famous Jugantar party. Later, he came
under the influence of Mahatma Gandhi and
Subhash Bose, and courted arrest many times.
In all, he has suffered imprisonment for 27 years in

various terms—the highest record in jail-going amongst all Congress leaders.

His longest incarceration was in connection with the historic Chittagong Armoury raid in 1930, for which he spent over nine years in jails and concentration camps in various parts of India. In 1940, he was again arrested and kept in jail for over six years. While still in detention, he was elected to the then Bengal Assembly in the 1946 elections as a Congress candidate. After Partition, he continued to be a member of the then East Bengal Assembly till 1954. He was a pioneer in organising the Pakistan National Congress in East Bengal, and was the General Secretary of the party and its parliamentary wing from the very beginning. He was also closely associated with the Bengali language movement begun in 1948, and because of his indignant protest against the killing of students on February 21, 1952 in Dacca, he was jailed for over two years.

In 1956, he joined the Awami League-Congress coalition ministry as Finance and Minority Affairs Minister. He was also the chairman of the provincial Minority Commission, constituted under the Nehru-Liaquat Pact of 1950. During the Ayub regime, he again suffered imprisonment and other forms of repression for about eight years.

Following the Pak military crackdown in March 1971, he went to India and engaged himself in organising resistance from Mujibnagar. He also served on the Consultative Council of the Bangladesh provisional government functioning from there. After liberation, he was made a member of the

National Militia Board of the Bangladesh Government, and was later appointed the first Bangladesh
Ambassador to Japan.

During my stay in Dacca, a meeting with Shri
Dhar was specially listed in my programme. The
reason was that of all of Sheikh Mujib's colleagues,
he is the only one who is not a regular member of
the Awami League; therefore, a talk with him, I
expected, would lead to a clearer view of the background of Bangladesh.

I had seen many a bust photograph of Shri Dhar
in the papers; nevertheless, seeing him in flesh, or
rather 'with all his flesh', was an exhilarating experience. He looks heavily-built, somewhat jovial
in expression, big, but not really plump. His dress,
like that of any Bengali bhadralok, is dhoti and
kurta. These are of pure khadi, for unlike many
others he is still a confirmed Gandhite. Though
around 70 now, he shows no signs of age in his
deportment; his appearance gives the impression of
perfect health, great erudition, and a sense of inner
fulfilment. With his self-confident bearing and
penetrating eyes, he looks every inch a veteran
politician. However, what charms and puts the
interviewer in instant communication with him is
the suggestion of a mischievous smile that flits across
his lips every now and then. Indeed, one cannot
but like him at first sight.

Formalities over, he at once launched into his
statement as if he had already divined the basic
purpose of my call on him : "So, you want to know
about the part played by our National Congress in
Bangladesh's struggle for freedom?" he said in

chaste Bengali. As I nodded assent, he went on:
"Well, then, listen carefully. Our Congress here,
which now calls itself the Bangladesh Jatiya Congress, is the oldest and the first secular nationalist
party in this country. All other parties here are
later growths, and practically all of them have
stemmed from the former All Pakistan Muslim
League. So, after the establishment of Pakistan,
our Congress was the only party which articulated
the call of nationalism and secularism in this country.
In the then Pakistan Constituent Assembly, the
first voice in support of the Bengali language too
was raised by a Congress member, Shri Dhirendra
Dutt. Later, when he returned to Dacca from
Karachi, he was accorded such a tumultuous welcome by the students here that even the hardened
communalists were bowled over. That was in 1948.
Ever since, in every popular movement in East
Bengal, launched either by students, labour or other
democratic sections, we Congressmen here have
extended our full support. True to our older
traditions, we strictly adhered to the principles of
nationalism and secularism even during the worst
days of Pakistani communal oligarchy. Had it
been possible for Pakistan to become one nation,
its Muslim majority making no difference, we
Congressmen would have had no objection to it.
But Pakistan, as constituted geographically and
racially, could never become one nation; even today
it is not one nation, as you are witnessing almost
everyday. But let us forget Pakistan for the time
being.

"Now, here in free Bangladesh, we are unconditionally committed to Bangladeshi nationalism and secularism. We Congressmen are absolutely not prepared to tolerate any discrimination on the basis of caste, creed, or religion. We are for Bangladeshi nationalism, and we are for independence, both of which we have gained after so much suffering and sacrifice.

Q: But, Sir, wouldn't it be correct to say that your Congress here was in practice reduced to a communal party of the Hindus only, since under the early Muslim League regime, perhaps not even a single Muslim remained in it?

A: Absolutely wrong. The Congress was never completely devoid of Muslim members; there are some even today. People of other communities have also been there. You must have heard of our very active and devoted Christian leader, Mr. Gomez. But that is really not the point. A party's policies should be judged not by its membership but by its principles and ideals. And the principles and ideals of the Congress have always been the same on the basis of which the founding fathers had established it, namely, nationalism, secularism, and freedom. Since, however, in Pakistan, the Government was unashamedly communal in character and it openly believed in theocracy, the greater part of mass grievance was naturally felt by the non-Muslims, among whom the Hindus of East Bengal were the most numerous. So, in practice, it did appear at times as if the Congress here was fighting only against the injustices being perpetrated on the Hindus, though in principle our fight against injustice was not confined to the

interests of any particular community. If you
go through the Assembly proceedings of the former
East Pakistan, you will find in them speeches
by our members demanding justice as much for
the poor Hindus as for the poor Muslims. For
example, you will see the debate on the Marriage
Bill, designed to give some protection to oppressed
Muslim women, in which it was our members who
had the courage to cross swords with the orthodox
mullahs. So, my dear friend, it is not correct to
say that the Congress here was ever reduced to a
Hindu party.

Q: The Awami League seems to have adhered,
more or less, to the same kind of principles as those
of the Congress. And, admittedly, this party has
proved itself to be the biggest nationalist party in
this country. As such, shouldn't it be conceded
that most of the credit for the triumph of secular
nationalism here, at least in principle, goes to it ?

A: No doubt, the Awami League is the biggest
and the most important political party in this
country, and its role in our struggle for freedom has
also been predominant and decisive.

But let us not forget that the Awami League too
was no more than a 'Muslim Awami League' in the
beginning, and its background was not nationalistic
but only an extension of that of the old Muslim
League.

To begin with, therefore, it was a communal
party. What made it secular? It was in fact the
sustained secular propaganda and secular behaviour
of the Congress, coupled with our joint struggle

for the Bengali language and the gradual realisation
on the part of the Awami League of concrete economic and political realities that eventually convinced
it of the need to drop the communal prefix and
become a secular Awami League. I have not the
slightest doubt that had the Congress not been
here, the needed psychological influence could not
have been exerted on the Awami League; and
perhaps the party might not have seen the necessity
to adopt a secular approach at all.

From the very beginning, we had the best of
relations with this party. Our leaders commanded
great respect and appreciation in their circles.
The Awami League nationalists were not unaware
of the great sacrifices we Gandhites had made and
the sufferings we had undergone for the emancipa-
tion of our country from foreign rule, and they
genuinely sympathised with us on that score. In
the 1954 General Elections, therefore, we worked
together, and, subsequently, on the basis of a 21-
point joint programme, we also participated in
Fazalul Haq's coalition ministry. In every democratic movement, launched by the Awami League,
we stood by it. During the anti-Ayub agitation
of 1969, all of us went to jail together. The Awami
League's movements were certainly nationalist
movements in their direction; so, there was no
reason for us not to co-operate.

Q: Should I take it then that now that you
have directly joined this government, you regard
the Awami League itself as an adequate substitute
for the National Congress, and that there is no

further need, in your view, for keeping up a separate
organisation of the Congress ?

A: I cannot say whether or not there is any
further need for keeping up the Congress organisation as such. Even as it is, there is hardly any
Congress organisation worth the name after the
Pak military crackdown of 1971, in which all its
offices and records were almost totally destroyed.
Still, as an old Gandhite, I would say only this that
after the attainment of freedom in 1947, Gandhiji
himself had advised the National Congress of your
country to dissolve itself as a ruling party and
assume the form and role of a Lok Sevak Sangh.
Of course, your Congress never paid any heed to
his advice.

But now, at least in Bangladesh, I believe that
our Congress workers here can certainly do a lot
of good by reorganising themselves into such a
Lok Sevak Sangh.   Besides, so far as party politics
and electioneering are concerned, I do not think
there is any alternative to the Awami League in
the present phase. And since our principles and
ideals are the same, there can be no question of the
Congress party playing the role of the opposition.

But so far as your suggestion about the Awami
League itself becoming, in effect, 'the National
Congress of Bangladesh,' is concerned, while, as I
said earlier, the principles and ideals of the two
parties are exactly alike, still there are some very
significant differences in their organisational set-
ups and orientation. Of course, behind all these
differences lies the specific history of this country
and of the two older organisations from which the two

parties have sprung. After all, the Awami League inherited the organisational set-up of the older Muslim League, which believed in the two-nation theory. Some of that inheritance is still clinging to the leadership of this party. Its old tendencies and methods of thinking and working cannot, therefore, vanish all of a sudden; these must necessarily take some time to wither away.

In fact, the main reason why I joined this government is that perhaps in the few years that are now left to me in this world, I may be able to do something towards fulfilling a part of that pledge which I signed in blood nearly fifty years ago as a mere lad of 13. That was to bring about a revolution in the life of my people.

Q: Some Congress leaders here are said to be unhappy about your joining the Government as an Awami Leaguer ? Is that correct ?

A: Absolutely wrong. None of my colleagues in the Congress has raised the slightest objection to this development. In fact, I have not even formally resigned from the Congress, nor has anybody asked for my resignation. All that has happened is simply this that the Awami League offered me its label, and I got elected unopposed. Thus, I do become a member of this party's parliamentary wing, but I am not yet a primary member of the party as such.

The truth is that I have joined the Government only in my individual capacity and on the personal insistence of Sheikh Saheb. After all, on the previous occasion, when he sent me to Tokyo as his

Ambassador, I was in no way associated with his party; still he entrusted me with some of the most delicate and secret diplomatic tasks in Japan. Therefore, with such trust being reposed in me by him, how could I decline his invitation to join his Government ?

Q: Some so-called Opposition parties here raise so much noise against India, to the extent even of maliciously linking the names of one or two persons in the Cabinet with the alleged imperialistic designs of India against your country. Yet I notice no publicity campaign on behalf of your Government to counter all this slandering, nor do I see any worthwhile effort to popularise the new concepts your Government has adopted as the fundamental principles of its state policy. May I know the reason for this slackness ?

A: I concede that your complaint is well-founded; there is indeed very little counter-propaganda here. Also, insofar as the basic ideals are concerned, obviously, only Sheikh Saheb himself has the stature to be able to propagate them without reserve ; the other leaders have perhaps still to acquire the courage to do that ! But the real reason for this state of affairs is again the same which I gave you in explanation of the organisational set-up of the ruling party, namely, its legacy of the past. The new ideas must necessarily take some time to make their impact, though everybody knows them, and the people have clearly voted in favour of them. As for malicious propaganda against some of us personally, we consider it below our dignity to take notice of it.   Our entire past and our present and future deeds are going to be the fittest reply.

Q: Now, how do you visualise the future, especially, the future of India-Bangladesh friendship ?

A: Very bright, indeed. I am perfectly sure that the independent existence of Bangladesh will succeed, and the basic principles adopted by it will also succeed. Our Bangladeshi nationalism will now play its positive role in the sub-continent. India-Bangladesh friendship will, therefore, remain unshakable, and will acquire more and more strength as we move ahead.

You see, in the final analysis, everything depends on common principles and common interests. And today, both in your country and in ours, all popular sections are agreed that democratic socialism is the only workable solution of our problems. Therefore, since we are agreed on principles, and our interests in the world are identical, you may rest assured that our friendship too will endure; it will withstand all the strains and stresses which politics inevitably brings in, and it will be further strengthened in the future.

But while I paint this rosy picture for you to divine much that I leave unsaid, I must also point out with great regret that India has committed many blunders in managing her relations with us. I do not want to go into details. But, as the bigger country, she has not been able to conduct herself with us on all occasions in the way and spirit she ought to have done. Some of her officers, in particular, made matters very difficult for us. Your

Government must learn to be more judicious in the selection of those it sends here.

Q: Lastly, may I know if there is, or has been, any contact or exchange between your Congress here and the one that rules my country?

A: Absolutely not. In fact, for all the miseries that we have had to suffer here both as a political party and as upholders of an ideology, your Indian National Congress is in no way less to blame than Pakistan itself. Believe me, considering the way they forgot us after throwing us to the Pakistani wolves, you would not have found any trace of us here after 24 years of Pakistani rule if we ourselves had not possessed the necessary guts and the will to survive. And even if Bangladesh had become free after we had perished, its form and content would have been entirely different. Therefore, if Bangladesh is not only free today but is also a staunch friend of India, most of the credit for bringing about that happy result must go to those handful of Congressmen here who fought every adversity.

Let me relate to you a story. Some time before liberation, an Awami League leader saheb was telling me that, considering the geographical position of Bangladesh, the need for her to maintain friendly relations with India was imperative. To which I replied: "My dear Sir, when we, the Congressmen here, had said this very thing to you after the establishment of Pakistan in 1947, you were the ones who called us 'traitors and Indian agents'; do you remember that?" At this, the repentant gentleman could only hang his head in shame.

CHAPTER 6

The Road of Revelations

NEWS BEGAN to appear in Bangladeshi newspapers during the first week of May 1973 that Maulana Abdul Hamid Khan Bhashani, the veteran leader of the pro-Peking National Awami Party, was soon to begin a fast unto death with his three demands, and that a party conference to chalk out a programme of mass action was going to be held at his village Santosh on May 5. Thus informed, I thought it advisable to get to the Maulana before those 'momentous events' broke on the scene and to put through my own little project of arriving at an understanding of his political philosophy. And so, on the morning of May 4, I set off for his village.

Santosh, the hamlet made famous by the Maulana, is situated some 60 miles north-west of Dacca in the district of Tangail, near the main town of that name. Buses ply up to Tangail, from where you can get a cycle-rickshaw for the further two miles down to the village. The road that links Dacca city with Tejgaon Airport runs further north and forks at Tongi, some 9 miles from the capital, the main highway leading to Mymensingh and north

Bangladesh and the other branch going to Tangail.
As I had taken the precaution of journeying back
to the city from Tejgaon and boarding the bus
from the main bus stand near the new railway
. station, I was able to occupy a seat from the very
beginning, and had, therefore, a less arduous journey
than it could otherwise have been.

But once on the move, the anticipated physical
jolts soon began to be pushed into the background
by the numerous mental shocks the road seemed to
hold in store for the over-vigilant observer. While
passing through the industrial town of Tongi, I
was greatly surprised and disappointed to notice
that practically every factory wore a completely
deserted look. Most were no more than gaping
sheds, with roofs blown off and scarcely any machinery inside. No smoke billowed out of any chim-
ney, though it was ten in the morning on a working
day. In the open enclosures too, there was no sign
of any activity or movement, nor of stock. On
the whole, the impression was overwhelming that
a complete standstill of all productive activity
obtained here, and that the factories as such were
no better than junk. Only at one mill did I notice
any workers, but they too seemed to be holding
some kind of a labour meeting at the gate, or were
perhaps on strike; and a person, presumably a union
leader, was busy keeping them warmed up by
waving his clenched fist in the air.

On seeing the most famous industrial area so
near the capital in such hopeless condition, I could
not but feel utterly disheartened and dejected.
Two or three different lines of thought crossed my

mind. First, with this level of industrial restoration right under its nose, how could the Government here be so brazen-faced as to claim that 99 per cent of industry had been restored all over the country, and that targets of production had been achieved to this or that percentage. Secondly, where was the question of any restoration at all when, in a single concentrated area like Tongi, no factory appeared to be equipped with any worthwhile machinery or stock. If this were the general state of disappearance of machinery all over the country, then one could safely put aside all hope of industrial recovery in this devastated land for at least the next five to seven years. Thirdly, what was the sense of waving clenched fists when all that remained to be shared was no more substantial than the medium in which the waving was being done ?

As the overloaded bus, panting and fuming, slowly lurched forward beyond Tongi, we came across a series of unrestored bridges—which gave the lie to another lot of Government propaganda. In all, on that 60-mile stretch of narrow road, I counted four major bridges under slow reconstruction—slow, because there was hardly any labour on the site—the bus had to cross over dry beds of the rivulets or the seasonal lakes at these places. An equal number of Bailey bridges were still in their positions as placed by the Indian military before their withdrawal, and these were apparently in use as normal bridges, for no reconstruction work had yet been taken in hand at these points. Thus, in 60 miles—and remember, this is the central capital area—eight major bridges were yet to be restored. Calculating on that basis, one can imagine how much credence can be lent to the Mujib Government's claim that 298 bridges out of 300 had been restored ! No one says that the Government should use a magic wand to restore all the blown-up bridges. But, at the same time, a responsible Government should not indulge in factual inexactitudes in order to minimise the importance of the work done in Bangladesh by the Indian Army. All that can be claimed truthfully is that some kind of a workable road communication has been restored between certain major towns, and that buses can ply during the dry months without much risk, if not overloaded. But the credit even for this partial restoration should go to the Indian military, whose engineers had placed huge Bailey bridges at all important crossings before bidding farewell to this country. This fact should be brought home to the Bangladeshi people.

During this journey through the countryside, the writer became aware of another aspect of life here, which had not till then been apparently noticed by any other observer. It is needless to point out that Bangladesh is not really 'a foreign country'. Being an integral part of East India, as it was also politically till 1947, it has the same natural and physical environment as the rest of this region. And from that point of view, an Indian, and particularly a Bengali, while moving about here, can scarcely feel that he is in a foreign country. It is the same cloud-laden sky, the same abundance of water, the same greenery—endless stretches of paddy fields broken here and there by a solitary

coconut, date or other palm tree, thick clumps
of bamboo overhanging innumerable little ponds
packed with large lotus leaves, and, at every few
thousand yards, a group of tin and mat sheds or
of those peculiar thatched huts with their rounded
and drooping corners, desperately clinging to either
side of the road like a small human bee-hive—all
this is here to remind the visitor that he is in Bengal.
Above all, the language and the script too are
here, leaving no room for doubt on that score. Yet,
despite so much in common, it doesn't take a
discerning observer long to discover that life here
does not possess even that simple order and tidiness
which is so striking a characteristic of most home-
steads in every village of our Bengal. Instead,
one sees here pervasive disquiet, disturbance, and
chaos in every habitation. It is not merely a
question of resources or material capacity. What
it calls attention to is the human outlook that is
at the back of it. And the kind of outlook one
sees reflected here in actual living points to a mind
to which life on earth seems to possess no value or
meaning at all. It is an indifferent, unreflecting
and unrespons ive mind. May be, the present
position is not all normal, being a part of the after-
math of the recen t upheaval. But the total impression one gets here is of a people who are not acquain-
ted in the least with the art of living. There is an
all-pervading ugliness and coarseness of texture
which imparts to the human environment here a
distinct character of its own, quite different from
ours.

Subsequently, on visits to the houses of some
middle-class, educated families in Dacca, I had the

same experience of coarseness and apathy in their
way of living. For example, if their sitting room
had some kind of modern furniture and curtains,
etc., there was always a visible layer of dust on
them. The container in which something to drink
was offered, bore clear signs of not having been
washed properly for weeks on end. In regard to
drinking water, particularly, a peculiar practice of
not washing the tumblers can be observed in almost
every wayside restaurant. All the tumblers are
placed in the middle of the table, and as these are
emptied, either fully or partially, they are again
filled up by the alert waterman; and groups of diners
come and go, drinking from the same, unwashed
and unchanged tumblers day after day.

In a similar fashion, a common trough, piled
up with rice, is circulated among the guests, and
though the trough is equipped with its own ladle,
the over-eager guests, intent on a second helping,
think it quite in order to strike the filled-up
ladle on the plate they are already eating from, to
jerk the sticky lumps down from it, and then to
insert the ladle back into the pile of rice. Thus
gathering minute particles of soiled residue from
innumerable used plates, the rice in the common
trough acquires an odour that makes it almost
impossible for a true Indian even to stand the
proximity of it, let alone think of eating it. Surely,
no one will say that this total ignorance of the most
elementary rules of health and hygiene is also an
abnormal situation, arising out of the recent upheaval and the present economic dislocation ?
Similarly, those who have any sense of living do
not allow dust to accumulate on their furniture

merely because conditions are not favourable. In fact, it is times like these when the values of a people can be truly judged and weighed.

*   *   *   *

During this bus journey, I also availed of the opportunity to study the collective reaction of the people here to an 'individual Indian'. The readable expressions on various faces and trends of the conversation that followed a full introduction, led only to one conclusion: the common people here have got into a love-hate complex with regard to India and the Indians. On one plane, they feel attracted and obliged to India, and, therefore, want to come nearer. But, on another plane, they have serious misgivings and deep-seated suspicions about Indian influences and designs, and, therefore, want to keep at as much a distance as possible. No doubt, what lie behind this complex are some old memories and, particularly, the Pakistani history of the past 25 years, during which they were taught only to hate and fear India and regard her as their worst enemy. But when the same hated and detested India came forward to deliver them from the Pakistani nightmare, this experience of concrete reality caused them no small amount of wonder and amazement. Every allegation that is levelled against India in Bangladesh today is only a reflection of a constant effort to make this experience intelligible and rational to large numbers of ignorant people. Since they must believe that India is the same pre-Partition 'Hindu zamindar' and that Indian intentions with regard to 'Musalmans' can never be above board, they must also find some ulterior objective behind all that India has done for their country. Some so-called opposition leaders, especially those who still have a soft corner for Pakistan, make use of this widespread confusion and unthinking adherence to fixed ideas for advancing their own prospects in the political field.

But, at the same time, many educated and intelligent persons with a sincere belief in the necessity of India-Bangladesh friendship also want to know as to what India's true intentions are with regard to their country. And since erstwhile East Pakistan by itself posed no military threat to India—rather its location right 'in the lap of India', as they put it, restricted the Pakistani threat even in the West, because Pakistan had a worry on her hands, of which she is now totally rid—an ordinary Indian's explanation that his country needed 'a friendly Bangladesh' to ensure the safety of its eastern frontiers does not wholly satisfy the inquisitive here.

*　　　　*　　　　*　　　　*

On the way to Santosh from the Tangail bus terminus, the rickshaw-wallah, having come to understand that 'a Dacca journalist' was going to meet the Maulana, started recounting his own tale of woe :

"What to say, babu," he began, slowing down on his pedals. "Ever since this 'azadi' has come, we poor people are only having our backs broken. In olden times, we made about five takas a day, but then rice was available at one taka a seer, and so, even after buying two seers of rice for the seven of us, we had three takas left for the other needs. But now, though we make eight takas a day, we need five for the rice only, and the remaining three takas take us nowhere. You see this lungi? It is a rag now. I bought it when the first elections were held, for five takas. Now a lungi like this costs twenty takas, quite beyond me. So, in another few days, I shall be as free as I was born, totally azad !"

"But your brethren in Dacca," I said, "are making fifteen to twenty takas a day. And the cinemas are so full of them that other people can't get in. We hear they also drink a lot of toddy !"

"Babu," he said, "only those can go after cinema and toddy who have no families to feed. But those who have eight persons in their hut to keep alive must look like me, in torn lungi and bare of body. For us poor people Pakistan was all right. At least, we had enough 'bhat' then to eat to our fill."

"If that is so," I said, 'then why did you run after the Awami League so much? Surely, it didn't win merely by the votes of the babus?"

"Only in the first elections did we do so," he said, "because its leaders made promises that they would get us rice at one taka a seer. But those promises are now forgotten."

"But the Awami League won the second elections too," I said.

"Allah alone knows how they did it," he said. "At least here, in Tangail, not even twenty in a hundred voted for it."

"May be, not in Tangail, but in the country as a whole, people certainly voted for it,"

"Allah alone knows!"

Thereupon I asked him a straight question: "So, according to you, no good has come out of this azadi?"

"Why not, a lot of good has come out," he said. "Have you not seen in Dacca how every leader has now got two bungalows and four cars? Where was all this merry-making in Pakistan? Why, nobody even knew who the hell they were. Even Sheikh Saheb himself went about on a bicycle."

"So, you don't have any trust even in Sheikh Saheb?" I asked.

"What is the use of having trust?" he countered. "Even if he is a good man, what can he do? What can a single good man do among a thousand thugs?"

"So, according to you, all these thugs are now looting the country?" I asked.

"Yes," he said, "all these thugs are looting the country, and along with them their friend India is also looting the country. Its military took away all the goods from here!"

At this I asked him cautiously: "India's military took away the goods—who said this to you?"

"Nobody needed to say this," he said, "for I saw it with my own two eyes. Here, at the nearby Jamna river, they loaded away everything on boat after boat."

"Brother," I said, "all that must have been the heavy arms of the Pakistani army."

"No," he said, "those were machines and vehicles, and a lot of paddy and jute!"

"Brother," I said. "Rice is two and a half takas a seer here, and only two rupees a kilo in the other Bengal. What fool would take rice from here and sell it in the other Bengal? You can think for yourself."

"Where is all the rice then?" he wondered loudly. "Government is giving us this rotten atta to eat. Can a man pull a rickshaw the whole day eating only atta? You will see, babu, all of us will be dead before the year is out."

"Don't worry," I consoled him. "Nothing of the kind will happen by eating atta. After all, the Pakistanis too ate only atta, and you must have seen how strong and healthy they were. Have faith in Allah. Everything will be all right."

"No, babu," he shook his head in despair. "Nothing will be all right. This country is now doomed. Still more rivers of blood will flow over this land."

In Tangail, the stronghold of Maulana Bhashani, only such talk could be expected from a poor, starving man; so, there was nothing surprising in what he said. Besides, what he said was not all wrong either; high living by political leaders in Dacca could be seen by anybody. They were presently busy marrying off their daughters, and thousands of guests were being entertained by them at these ceremonies. I had occassion to observe some of them, and was amused at finding another proof of the identity of class interests between the Awami League and our Congress, Syndicate or Indicate. Yet I felt elated by the thought that this poor man, beyond repeating the usual charge of ransacking against the Indian Army, had not uttered a single word against the Indian people as such, although he had not the slightest idea of the true identity of his fare. On the contrary, referring to India on several occasions, he had used the epithet 'Mahan Bharat'. " 'Mahan Bharat' is doing this, what a shame," etc. Again, while crossing one or two bridges on the way, he had occasion to praise the very Indian Army he was running down. "Indian jawans paid us full wages for every work they took from us, but the Pakistanis before them hardly ever paid us our dues . . .", etc. In short, any possible 'return to Pakistan' was opposed even by that poor rickshaw-wallah. Today, in Bangladesh, Pakistan is remembered very much in the same way as the British are remembered in India.

———

CHAPTER 7

Encounter with the Maulana
at Santosh !

MAULANA BHASHANI'S new house is situated almost
at the very mouth of the village; it is a group of
three or four mud-and-mat huts, with a mat-screen
around, fencing in the dwelling from the outer
world. His old house is said to have been burnt
down by the Pakistani Army. A few steps in front
of the house runs the link road from Tangail, with
a rectangular, small lake running parallel to it on
the other side and a complex of old, dilapidated
feudal mansions lining the far bank of the lake.
These buildings belonged to the former zamindars of
Santosh, who were known here as the 'rajas'. It
is said the last Raja, while migrating to India after
Partition, had handed over these mansions to the
Maulana with an express wish that he could use
them for any public purpose he deemed fit. The
Maulana had been running some kind of a college
here; a high school can still be seen in one of the
outer buildings. He is further said to have tried,
through recourse to the Pakistan Supreme Court, to
have these properties declared as the legitimate

heritage of some neo-Muslim family. The case was thrown out. Subsequently, it seems, these buildings slipped out of his hand ; and the Mujib Government has now established some of its revenue offices here.

Some people say that one of the reasons for the Maulana's vituperations against the new regime is his loss of control over these properties. He is reported to have nurtured the idea of establishing an Islamic University here. But the real position is not clarified either by the Maulana or by any Government spokesman. Thus the mystery of the mansions of Santosh remains as unsolved as the personality of the Maulana himself.

Having announced in the arrival of 'a newsman from Dacca', the rickshaw-wallah had left. Presently, the Maulana appeared from behind the mat-screen, attired, as usual, in his loose-sleeved, long *kurta* and *lungi*, both garments seeming to need a fresh wash. In photographs, the Maulana somehow conveys the impression of height, but actually he is short-statured, though heavily-built. Only two of his features are prominent and obtrusive enough to attract immediate attention: one is his mane-like beard, which hangs down to his chest like a double-edged broom, and the other is, of course, his belly, which is colossal. Like other Bangladeshi leaders, the Maulana too takes great delight in showing off his powers of expression in classical Bengali.

By profession, he is a 'pir'; therefore, he has all the attributes of this species of religious men— rosary in hand, 'pan' in mouth, collyrium in the eyes. However, his family and social background is known only to a few close associates; the Maulana himself talks little about it. All that is known is that years ago he used to run a firewood depot somewhere in Assam, presumably in Sylhet, dabbling, at the same time, in some religious hocus-pocus. Later, he wandered all over India for many years, during which period he is said to have taken regular lessons at the Islamic Institute of Deoband in U.P., under the guidance of the famous Hussain Ahmed Madani. Thus he became a full-fledged Maulana.

In politics, he is said to have been a revolutionary in the beginning, as all youngmen of Bengal at his time were. Then he became a Congressite, finally ending up, some time before Partition, as a Muslim Leaguer. During Partition, he played a leading role in getting the district of Sylhet ceded to Pakistan. Later, in Pakistan, he separated from the Muslim League, and became the President of the East Pakistan Awami League. In 1957, he came out of the Awami League too, and formed his own National Awami party, which also split in 1966, leaving him the President of its so-called pro-Peking group.

Despite this background, or rather because of it, his true political line is still a puzzle. He is, no doubt, a mysterious person, and one of his special pleasures seems to be to deepen the mystery all the time. Some people say that he is secretly a Maoist communist, and that his religious mendicancy is only a means of livelihood or possibly just a cover. Others hold him as nothing more or less than a charlatan and an opportunist, for whom all that matters is personal publicity, for it is only through publicity that his business as 'pir' flourishes. On a purely secular plane, he can be compared to Ram Manohar Lohia or Kamaraj Nadar of India. However, he has changed his colour so many times in his life that it is almost impossible to give any final verdict about him. All his ideas, insofar as he expresses them, show a tremendous amount of confusion and inconsistency.

In any case, he was not lacking in courtesy; he was still more pleased to know that his visitor had come not just from Dacca but from Delhi. Complaining about some gastric trouble he was having, he led the way inside, beckoning me to follow, and seated himself in an outer hut on the left, meant presumably for visitors. (Incidentally, the Maulana's political hunger-strikes are so timed as to fit in with the treatment schedule of his gastric trouble.)

In the midst of his opening lecture, he got up and went out, procured some fruits from somewhere, cut and peeled them himself, and came back, bearing the fruit-pieces on a plate, along with a bowl full of porridge. All this he did in the writer's full view.

Asking me to help myself, he again sat down and resumed his speech, flaring up now and then, wherever he encountered any objection to his line of argument. During all this time, I did not notice any other man or personal servant near him, except for a small boy of about eight, who kept whining and whimpering about lack of food. The household being subject to purdah, I did not see any woman about. The outward simplicity of the Maulana's way of living is, of course, undeniable.

The interview was conducted entirely in Bengali; the Maulana would on no account agree to converse in Urdu with one who could speak his language. In fact, noticing that I took notes in the Urdu script, he had his first blow-up: "You, a Bengali, write in Urdu?" he burst out. "You ought to be ashamed of yourself!"

"Maulana," I put in, "it is only a form of shorthand. Besides, here in your country, I am not exactly 'Bengali'. Here, I am only a Bengali-speaking Indian. That is how it is entered in my passport!"

This made him angrier. "Your passport is all wrong", he thundered. "There is no such thing as 'an Indian'. India is a group of nations, among whom the most homogeneous are the Bengalis. The Bengalis are a nation; they have always been a nation. Their absolute attachment to their language, the literature, philosophy and politics that have taken shape in the moulds of that language, are the common heritage of all Bengalis. Look at your history, beginning from 1890. The Bengalis never believed in the so-called non-violence of Gandhi, nor did Gandhi and his Congress ever repose any trust in the Bengalis. During the entire history of the Congress, only two Bengalis were elected to its Presidentship, and both of them were thrown out unceremoniously.

"The youth of Bengal have always taken to the path of struggle and revolution, and, following it,

they have gone to the gallows in their thousands
with 'Long live the Revolution' on their lips. Thus,
there is ample proof to show that Bengal is an
entity by itself, with an ideology of its own, a soul
of its own. It cannot form part of any other country
or nation; it is a nation by itself. And that is why
I believe that your Bengal too will in the near
future liberate itself from the clutches of India in the
same way as our Bengal has already done so from
those of Pakistan. And the two will unite and
form Greater Bengal."

"But, Maulana," I objected, "you speak of
'Muslim Bengal'. How then can our Bengal be
interested in your scheme ?"

"I have never spoken of Muslim Bengal," he
said. "It is the newspapers which impute such
things to me. Tell me, why should I say 'Muslim
Bengal'? What is the necessity for me ? I am
85 per cent here in my Bengal today ; I (Muslim)
shall still be about 70 per cent in Greater Bengal.
As such, why should I worry ? Of course, if you
speak of your Bengal as 'Hindu Bengal', that would
be justified, because it is the minority that needs
protection, not the majority. Tell me, do you
ever call your Hindustan 'Hindu Hindustan' ?
Why should you ? Where is the necessity for you?
The very name 'Hindustan' is derived from you;
it is nothing but 'Hindu.' Similarly, the Bengali
nation as a whole is largely 'Muslim.' Now, it is
for you, the Hindus of Bengal, to think and decide
whether you stand to gain some thing by coming
along with me. When you finally discover that

it would do you good, you would certainly come to me. Let me give you an example :

"Very recently you saw that our people here carried your Army on their backs to Dacca. Just imagine, what would have happened if you had come here with your Army in 1947 itself ? Why, your Army would have had to advance to Dacca over the dead bodies of these very people. From this one example, it should be clear that people do not hesitate to come together if it serves some vital interest of theirs. All the Bengalis will likewise come together when they see their interest in it."

"And what about your Islamic socialism ?"

"It is only socialism plus Islam. It only means that I do not exclude my religion from my socialism. No good person ever excludes his religion from his politics. Tell me, if purely Hindu parties in your country, like the Congress and the Jana Sangh, can have Muslim members, why can't I have Hindu members in my Islamic socialism ? Should your Muslims ever come to the conclusion that it would serve their interests better if, instead of the Congress or the Jana Sangh, they joined the Hindu Mahasabha—would they not go there?

"You have the Aligarh Muslim University and the Jamia Milia, etc. The very names suggest that these are Muslim institutions. But who are educated there ? Seventy per cent Hindu students. Why ? Because it serves them well. Do these Hindu children become Muslim because they get their education in Muslim institutions ? So, what is not a sin in your Delhi or Aligarh cannot possibly

be a sin in my Islamic University at Santosh.
How can Hindu children become Muslim here ?
Do Muslim members of your Congress or Jana
Sangh become Hindus? I myself remained in the
Congress for 18 years. Did I become a Hindu ?

"The trouble really is that you Hindus have
never taken the Muslims to your heart. Had you
done so, there would have been neither any Partition, nor Pakistan. The whole world knows that
98 per cent of Muslims here have descended from
Hindu ancestors. Those of your Moulvis who tell
the Muslims in your country that their forefathers
were Arabs and Turks, of whose conquests they
should be proud, are simply misleading and ex-
ploiting the poor Muslims. But what was the
position of your Gandhi ? He would go on a fast
unto death even if one Harijan were converted to
Islam. That was the reason why one homeland
had to split into two, and now into three. Had the
Muslims been given even 13 per cent reservations at
the Centre at a certain juncture in our history,
there would have been no Partition.

"Why do I say 'Islamic socialism'? Because
I saw that those who, following the path of Marx,
forsook God, also gave up the path of humanity.
Today, the atheist communists of Russia and
China are displaying a degree of hatred and animo-
sity between themselves, in comparison to which
their hatred even for their traditional enemies has
paled into insignificance. Today, you can see
how the war-hating communists are fighting the
bitterest war among themselves."

"But, Maulana," I objected again, "the record

of Islam too doesn't appear to be any more glorious.
Hasn't there been continuous bloodshed in the name
of Islam ? Aren't Muslim nations shedding each
other's blood even today ?"

"All this history has nothing to do with Islam,"
he said. "This is only the usual story of imperialism
with the Islamic label, just as the imperialism of the
West had the Christian label. Except in the first
few years, the tenets of Islam have never been
strictly followed. Islam is a Dharma, and Dharma,
in our language, means 'that which you hold on to'
for survival on this earth. Therefore, if any religion
leads to a massacre of humanity, that is not religion,
but irreligion."

"But, Maulana, aren't there serious hazards in
conducting politics in the name of religion? You
just now alluded to the way Islam became just
another form of imperialism."

"Not at all," he said. "Misuse of religion is
not religion, and it does not in the least detract
from the importance of religion, just as quackery
does not minimise the importance of medicine.
The truth is that all good politics has to be conducted
on the basis of religion. Take the great men of
our Bengal—from Rammohan Roy to Tagore—
each one of them did great things because he took
his stand on the basis of religion. No great purpose
can be accomplished without recourse to religion."

"It seems, Maulana, you are giving an altogether
new interpretation of religion?"

"Not at all," he said. "I am only telling you
what religion means. Now, a group of mullahs

came to me some time ago. They said, 'you are propagating socialism; that is *kufr*, because God has promised to provide every living thing on earth with fixed sustenance, you cannot change an iota of it by any new division of wealth, and that all the five fingers can never be equal,' etc. I told them : 'It is fourteen hundred years since the Koran was revealed. Man, on this earth, may still live for another fourteen hundred or, may be, fourteen thousand years. So, for fourteen thousand years, man will have to carry on with this one Koran; another will never be given. But would its revelations be understood and acted upon in the same way as now for all those fourteen thousand years?' I told them, 'you shed many a tear over the 33 crore devatas of the Hindus. But what is your own condition ? Every despotic and immoral monarch, every sensuous and profligate nawab, and the corrupt ministers of today—these are your devatas, and you worship at their altars every day. That is all the Islam you have got. So, my socialism plus God is a declaration of war against you too.' At this they pronounced me *kafir* and went away.

"Now let me tell you this: that my God is not the God of any particular religion; He is the God of Man. Therefore, you can as well describe my philosophy by saying that it is Socialism plus Man."

"Very good," I said, wanting to change the subject. "Now, would you kindly give me an indication of any proof that you may have in support of your oft-repeated charge that India alone is responsible for the present economic plight of

Bangladesh, and that Marwaris are infiltrating into your economy and looting your country ?"

"I have one thousand and one proofs," he said. "But if any one thinks that I am indulging in baseless allegations, well, let there be a joint Commission of four judges, two from your Supreme Court and two from ours, and let this Commission go into the question and fix responsibility. Should it hold me a perjurer, I would be prepared to undergo any punishment."

"This is sheer advertising, Maulana," I commented. "Why don't you straightaway publish the names of those Marwaris who have set up their business here after liberation ?"

At this the Maulana flew into a real rage and burst upon me like a tempest: "You dare cross-examine me ?" he roared. "I thought you were a Bengali, but you have turned out to be an agent of the Marwaris themselves ! Without doubt, some Marwari seth must have sent you to me !"

"Maulana," I said coolly, "You are wasting your breath for nothing. I am only trying to find out the truth. I am in Dacca; you give me the addresses of four Marwaris who have entrenched themselves here after Independence. I will check up myself, and publish their names in the Indian papers."

"You will publish their names in the Indian papers ?" he asked sarcastically. "Which one of them is not owned by the Marwaris, pray ? I say one thousand Marwaris have fanned out throughout Bangladesh. I wrote to Indira, telling her that

India-Bangladesh friendship would end because of the Marwaris. How unfortunate that the same India, which did so much for us, should sneak into our house like a thief and plunder us! I was kept under house-arrest for full nine months in India, yet I never uttered a word of complaint because at that time India was discharging its duty to my country as a friend. It is for the sake of this friendship that I demand the setting up of a joint Commission of enquiry.

"Let there be no mistake about it: the Marwaris are leeches; they are sucking the blood out of both Bengals. But since you are still under the spell of their wealth and power, you continue to wallow in your present state of servility and call it 'Indian Nationalism'. But let me tell you again; indeed, I prophesy that within five years, your Bengal will embark on a mass struggle to free itself from the domination of India, and within twenty years, my dream of a Greater Bengal will come true. Of course, I shall not be living till then to see the fulfilment of my life-long mission, but many of you will witness these events within their life-time."

As he started to leave with his prophetic declaration still ringing in the air, I asked him : "While on this, would you like to make two more prophecies ? One, about the future of your Biharis, and the other about that of the Hindus here ?"

"To the Biharis," he said, "I had given the warning in 1947 itself that they must not come here as the population in these parts had already crossed the saturation point. Still, to those who came I gave the advice that they should assimilate themselves with the Bengalis and must on no account try to become their overlords or capitalists. But, to their misfortune, they acted in the opposite direction. On the one hand, egged on by their Pakistani masters, they opposed Bangladesh, and, on the other, they fattened themselves on the sweat and blood of the poor Bengalis. Thus it became all the more difficult to bring about any fraternization between the two communities, and the whole Bengali-Bihari question assumed the colour and dimensions of an open class war—a war between the few haves and the mass of the have-nots, a war for economic rights of a people in their own homeland. It is thus their own shortsightedness that has brought the Biharis to their present pass.

"The solution of their problem now lies in transferring as many of them to Pakistan as the number of Bengalis we must get back from there and resettle here. As for the rest, they can go back to India, where they rightly belong. Mujib himself had brought them over by touring around your Bihar; therefore, he should now make arrangements for sending them back to their original homes.

"As for the Hindus here, I have for them the same advice: they must take a lesson from the fate of the Biharis and consciously avoid all those mistakes that the latter committed. Where is communalism in all this? The Hindus are my people, and I love them as much as I love the Muslims. I have 'mureeds' (disciples) both among the Hindus and the Muslims. Even so, I admit that some people propagate communalism from my platform. But the reason for this aberration is electioneering politics. I do not contest any elections myself. But all my associates are not saints; they have an eye on some kind of elective office. But are they the only ones in this game? Mujib himself would use every trick of communalism to keep himself in power. In fact, he is the worst communalist this country has ever produced. Why, he was not even prepared to drop the prefix 'Muslim' from the name of the Awami League. It was I who reformed that name. It was I who built up the Awami League. It was I who first gave the slogan of Independent Bangladesh. It is again I, who am raising the voice of Greater Bengal. I am always the first . . ."

As I left some time later, I ran again into the Maulana, standing on the roadside and, as usual, waxing eloquent in classical Bengali. The farewell talk turned to the old mansions along the far bank of the lake, and on being asked to whom the mansions belonged presently, he said: "These now belong to bats and jackals, and snakes and scorpions have turned them into their living quarters. A full panchayat could be held here if only the fifth member were also present—Mujib himself!"

From this style of language, it is not difficult to infer the true reason for all the frustration and bitterness the Maulana displays at 92. It is nothing more than his desire for recognition and honour, especially from those who hold the strings of power. The Maulana believes that no man should ascend the throne, in his Bangladesh at least, without first touching his feet. And it has

to be conceded that this desire on the part of the
Mahatma—I mean, the Maulana—is not altogether
unnatural. He did have as much hand, subjectively
that is, in promoting the prospects of Sheikh
Mujib in Bangladesh as in India that comparable
old fogey, Kamaraj Nadar, had in contriving the
installation of Indira Gandhi as Prime Minister
on the first occasion.

CHAPTER 8

'Operation Telephone Diplomacy !'

IN GOVERNMENT publications of Bangladesh, Prime Minister Sheikh Mujibur Rahman is variously described as 'a living legend', 'a unique charisma', 'an institution by himself', 'an inseparable part of the emotional existence of $7\frac{1}{2}$ crore 'Bengalis', 'Amar Neta, Tomar Neta', Mujib Bhai, and, above all, Banga Bandhu—the last often used by Sheikh Saheb himself. When he has to say 'I', he very often says: 'Now, Banga Bandhu is addressing you', etc.

There is not the slightest doubt that Sheikh Mujibur Rahman's position in Bangladesh today is very akin to that occupied by Jawaharlal Nehru in India immediately after Independence. The comparison becomes still more significant when we remember that even for his political philosophy and day-to-day tactics, the Sheikh today looks more towards the late Pandit than towards anybody else. Like those of Panditji, all of Sheikh Saheb's colleagues too are so inferior to him both in status and calibre that for a Tajuddin Ahmed or Nazarul Islam, to dream of becoming the Prime Minister during his life-time is just out of the question. Therefore, every foreign journalist or writer who comes to Bangladesh has a desire to meet such an unrivalled and charismatic leader. It was so with this scribe too. Besides, I had two specific items of business with him. One was to get his autograph on an award-winning Hindi book of mine, with a view to promoting its prospects for further publication, and the other was a brief questionnaire in connection with the present work. Of course, for these two minor tasks, a personal interview was not required, nor did I press for one. I just left the book and the questionnaire with the P.M.'s Secretary in Gono Bhawan with the request that as soon as the job was done, I was to be called up. On the first day, I was told that the matter was so small that there could hardly be any hitch in getting it done.

But when, after receiving no word for four days, I went back to the P.M.'s Secretariat, enquiring, I was told that the matter was of high importance, and that there was indeed a hitch, a serious one. The Press Secretary to P.M., Mr. Amin-ul-Haq Badshah, gave me this piece of news : "We regret that answers to your questionnaire cannot be given, because you have come here without getting clearance from the Foreign Ministry of your Government."

Aghast, I represented: "Dear Sir, what is this great thing 'clearance'? You know I am a writer. I possess a valid passport issued by the President of my country and a valid visa issued by your High Commission in Delhi. I have come to your country on a visit. I am your guest. As I look around studying men and affairs, I take the opportunity to put a few questions to your Prime Minister. To answer or not to answer them is a matter that rests entirely on the discretion of your Prime Minister. How does my Government come into all this? "

"No !" Mr. Badshah said emphatically. "You must go to your High Commission and get a clearance. If they say that your questions can be accepted, we shall have no difficulty in dealing with them."

Thereupon, I said: "Do you realise what impression you are giving me ? And if my questionnaire is not answered, do you know what impression I shall carry back with me ?"

To this, Mr. Badshah gave this reply: "I do not care what impression you carry back with you. But your Government insists that we do not entertain Indian journalists without its approval."

"Very good !" I said. "If that be your condition, I will get you a certificate from the High Commission too. But it is really strange that your Prime Minister would not consent to take a decision on his own on so small a matter."

"You are unnecessarily complicating the issue," he said. "From your book, you appear to be 'the right kind of person'. So, why don't you get a word put in from the High Commission?"

"I will do that rightaway," I said, and took leave.

Somewhat heated up, I came down to the gate and paused at the outer Recepn toort cool myself,

Right then, a big, black, sleek Mercedes-Benz limousine, the like of which would cost about Rs. two lakhs in India today, came up from inside the courtyard and slowly glided past the gate. As it did so, the entire armed guard along the driveway clicked their heels and saluted. Inside the car, on the back seat, a somewhat fair-complexioned and good-looking high officer in costly gold-epauletted military uniform sat in majestic pose. The whole scene made an ineffaceable mark on my mind.

Greatly impressed, I asked the receptionist: "Who was the military man? Some Russian General?"

"No," came the reply. "He is our Air Chief".

"Oh!" I exclaimed. "But he looked as if Marshal Zukov himself had come back from the grave !"

"What ?"

"I say, how many planes are there in your Air Force ?"

"What ?"

"I mean, there must be a dozen or so, aren't there ?"

"Yes, may be more, may be less."

"Well," I concluded. "If that was your Commander of an Air Force of *twelve* planes, in that Mercedes, how would he pass through this gate when he had twelve thousand—Eh ?"

Bangladeshi people, generally, have little sense of humour. So, the poor fellow just blinked and blinked.

Next day, I looked up the High Commission. These offices are situated in the Dhanmandi residential area, which is in the western half of new Dacca. Prime Minister Sheikh Mujib's personal house, which was then having another storey added to it, is also in the same area. The Indian High Commission here is housed in five or six mansions in a row ; the rent alone would be not less than Rs. 25,000/- per month. The volume of the other recurring expenses on the inert and live furnishings in these mansions, is anybody's guess.

However, I had business only in one particular mansion, which stands on another road and houses the Information and Education Wing of the High Commission. But here, contrary to expectation, staff and furnishings were rather on the sparse side. The building itself did not have the tricolour on its mast; in fact, the mast itself was missing. Nor was there any photo-display or exhibit suggesting publicity, at the gate or in the lobby, to reassure the perplexed visitor that he is really at an Information Centre of the Republic of India. On the contrary, the building itself has a ghostly appearance, and the atmosphere inside has that uncanny touch of the unknown, the lurking, one instinctively associates with a secret service den. One feels one is stepping into a snare.

On enquiry about publications, all that was handed out was a poorly-produced paltry pamphlet, purporting to tell the story of India-Bangladesh co-operation during the first year of the latter's Independence. In effect, there was no story of co-operation; the pamphlet simply contained some facts and figures concerning the supply of goods and money by India to Bangladesh during that period. No other publication of any value could be spotted there, not even a poster or a wall calendar.

It was indeed intriguing to reflect on the functions of the wing. What does it do here ? What are all these people paid for ? Are there any lists of students who are in the process of exchange ? How many and what books have reached here from India, and been distributed ? Any books from Bangladesh to India ? What is the situation in regard to exchange of newspapers and periodicals ? Any Indian documentaries placed on the TV and the cinemas here ? What Indian speakers have so far been invited besides Maulana Asad Madani of the Jamiat ? etc. You can't get a satisfactory reply to any question at this Indian Information Office in Dacca.

Newspapers in this country carry concocted stories against India almost every day. Yet one rarely sees a contradiction or an explanatory press note issued by this office. There is a host of matters about which the Bangladeshi people are not aware of the correct facts. And while the so-called opposition leaders would naturally utilise the confusion to serve their own ends, the Mujib Government too prefers to keep mum about them; it has neither the courage nor the desire to lay bare the actual facts. But what prevents the Indian High Commission in Dacca from coming out with the truth ? Why should India be so tongue-tied in Bangladesh ?

There is a long list of allegations against the victorious and resplendent Indian Army. There is the complicated question of the destruction of bridges, factories, and communications. There is the disappearance of machinery and plant on a large scale. There are insidious allegations of palming off sub-standard goods and profiteering by India. There is the ghost of the allegedly surplus Nasik-printed notes still to be laid to rest finally. There are persistent rumours of Marwari infiltration, despite lack of evidence. And, above all, there is the crowning feat accomplished by 'the two hundred thousand armed guerillas' of the Mukti Bahini, in just vanishing !

Leave that aside. What are these diplomats of ours doing in the way of propagating the life and ideology of India itself in this country ? Nothing. In all of Dacca, you will see only one small, black signboard, hanging at the foot of a second storey room with the legend that this place is an 'Indian Information Centre'. Even this has its doors closed lest some inquisitive but mistaken Bangladeshi should come up there and disturb the sleeping chowkidar. But what really makes a publicist furious is the complete absence of any Indian display in this nation's capital. It is not at all a question of money. For, those who have the capacity to hire a whole row of five mansions for their comfort, can very well hire a biggish hoarding at some suitable place or a whole wall for the display.

Today in Dacca, every important country has put up its national display, depicting the life of its people, its beauty, and its products. The only one that seems to be missing is that of India, the closest friend of Bangladesh. India has so much to show to the people here. But all that is shown is through the commercial pamphlets of the Indian Air Lines Corporation, depicting, of all things, Ajanta and Ellora. These tracts too are just pinned up in the Hotel Inter-Continental, where not even one per cent of Bangladeshis can ever hope to step in.

The truth is that mass publicity can suggest itself only to those who have a stake in, and desire for, establishing direct contact with the bulk of the people in a country. But our High Commission in Dacca seems to believe that there is no such thing as a 'people of Bangladesh'. All that matters and is required, they seem to feel, is that contact is maintained with a handful of top men in the Government. That too, at long distance. Thus, all our diplomacy here seems to begin and end with the telephone. That is to say, we have only to lift the receiver and tell the concerned person what to do, and the necessary orders will have been issued before the receiver is placed back !

No doubt, such orders are being issued today, and will continue to be issued for some time more. But our 'Rajahs' here must not forget that after a certain period all these fiats and edicts of theirs will boomerang on them with re-doubled force. Virtually every leader of standing here hinted of this to me in many subtle ways, and at least one Awami League leader, putting aside politeness for a while, warned specifically and frankly:

"Bhai Saheb," he said, "we have no option today but to keep quiet. But let me tell you, the time is coming when for all your current high-handedness and brow-beating, you will have to repent in leisure. Just wait for some kind of a patch-up between us and the Pakistanis to materialise—recognition and all that, China, UNO, etc.—and then you will see that we are quite capable of giving you tit for tat."

The worst mistake that is being made is in the political field. The whole world knows that to rely solely on the ruling party in a democracy is the hallmark of foolish governments. Wise nations are those which more than with any party, ruling or otherwise, try to establish direct rapport with the common people of the countries they want to befriend. All this is so simple as really not to merit mention. Yet, from the conduct of our diplomats in Dacca, one would think that the Awami League is going to rule Bangladesh till doomsday. Except for a few top leaders of this party, none else is encouraged or even allowed by our diplomats to come near them. The result is that the Bangladeshi people as a whole have no clear idea or understanding of the nature of their relationship with India. There seems to be an all-round conspiracy of silence to keep the people confused, bewildered and befogged. The ultimate outcome is not going to be good. Meanwhile, when facts are not known, the people here are quite justified in believing the most fantastic tales about India and her intentions.

Our rulers seem to think that as long as a friendly country is kept well supplied with aid material and loans, and fabulous gifts are despatched with every emissary for the heads of that country, the hot-house garden of mutual friendship will remain ever green and flowering, immune from the vagaries of the political weather. Some such hopes were entertained by the USA too in India for many years after Independence. But the whole world saw to what unbelievable depths of despair those soaring hopes finally gave place towards the end of 1971. After aiding and helping India to the tune of some billions of dollars, the USA had to despatch its Seventh Fleet to the Bay of Bengal, in a move that could not be described as friendly. And today, to re-establish the almost broken links between them, the two countries are apparently engaged in exerting all the ingenuity and diplomatic skill they are capable of, but so far with little success.

What is intended to be conveyed by all this is very simple. To take any country's friendship for granted is the height of naivete in the present-day world. It is so straight and simple a thing that even to mention it seems an insult to intelligence. Yet that is exactly the mistake India is committing in Bangladesh today—that of taking a free country's friendship for granted. And, therefore, one feels the final outcome of this friendship is not going to be any different from the present state of India's relations with most of her neighbours.

But to resume the story: when after the distressing experience at the High Commission, an appointment with the Information Counsellor, Mr. S. Banerjee, eventually materialised, it was clear from the start that the basic line of communication was missing. An unfortunate misunderstanding had already taken root in the Prime Minister's

Secretariat and during the early rounds of the Chancery. So, even before hearing the full story, the diplomat queried: "How do we know who you are ? Why have you come here ? What do you write ?" etc., etc.

I represented: "Dear Sir, I have come here in connection with a family interest. But at the same time, unfortunately, I happen to be a writer by profession. So, while I am here, I am also collecting some material for a book that, I hope, will go to serve the same end which is the common objective of us all."

"All right," he said. "You leave some of your books here. We shall have them examined and, in due course, form some opinion."

A man in a foreign country, in normal circumstances, must necessarily consider himself a prisoner of his Government. Therefore, suppressing the wave of indignation that rose in me at this affrontry of 'forming an opinion,' I quietly left the two books I had actually brought for him as a gift and departed.

The crassness of all small men in power is really astounding. They expect to prevent an observer from reporting what he has to report, by withholding information and putting up barriers. Years of work in the field has taught us that only by disseminating knowledge and understanding can the people's minds be influenced. But our rulers seem to think that the best way to gain adherents to their line of thinking is to have books 'examined' and 'opinion on acceptability formed' in smug self-satisfaction.

The result was, of course, a foregone conclusion. After what had already taken place, a telephone call from the High Commission for the questionnaire to be answered would have been tantamount to confirming in practice what the highly sensitive writer had already described as 'telephone diplomacy'. Therefore, during the remaining five days in Dacca, no word came either from the high High Commission or from the castle-like Gono Bhawan. Weeks after return to Delhi, a letter arrived from Dacca with the news that 'the High Commission regrets that the Prime Minister is too pre-occupied to attend to the questionnaire.' It was suggested that I had better decide to do without this subject-matter in my projected work.

Now, on looking back on the rough draft of the questionnaire still in my papers, I can see why both the PM's Secretariat and the High Commission didn't want it answered, why they found silence more convenient as well as safer.

The questionnaire I had submitted to the Bangladesh Prime Minister's Secretariat was as follows :—

India-Bangladesh Friendship

1. Would those in Bangladesh, who oppose India-Bangladesh friendship, sleep more comfortably if this friendship were not present ?

2. Could it be hoped, in view of the expanding spheres of India-Bangladesh co-operation, that the present restrictions on travel and communication between the two countries would prove to be of temporary nature ?

3. Would your Government like to have any

special relationship with the Government of West Bengal, in the spheres of language, culture, education, and the fine arts ?

4. How far do you find the Indian experience in planned development and economic administration applicable and useful in the conditions in your country ?

Pakistan

5. What kind of relations would you like to have with Pakistan after the latter's recognition of Bangladesh ?

6. Could you visualise a situation in which the intended exchange of population between Bangladesh and Pakistan might become redundant ?

7. Must there be a war-crimes' trial even after Pakistan recognises Bangladesh and repatriates Bangladeshis on demand ?

8. Could your Government not give another chance to those in Bangladesh who are said to have opted for Pakistani citizenship, to make a fresh choice ?

Minorities

9. Since the success of secularism both in India and Bangladesh will be measured by the satisfaction of the respective minorities, would it do any good if a joint commission to look into minority grievances, is set up ?

10. Keeping in view the special affection the people of West Bengal have for the people of Bangladesh, could there not be a common formula for the

removal of minority grievances among the Bengali-speaking people, at least ?

*   *   *

To conclude this unhappy chapter, it is really sad to reflect how those in power have still to appreciate that to ask questions is the prerogative of the analyser as to refuse to answer them is that of the subject. But he must refuse, not take refuge.

CHAPTER 9

The Tragic Tale of The 'Biharis'

PERHAPS NO other class of people in the world today is as ruined, economically and socially, as smitten and smashed up as the community of the former Indian refugees in Bangladesh who are known here by the general term 'Bihari'. They acquired this nomenclature because most of them had come originally from Bihar and Eastern U.P. Generally, however, the term is supposed to include all those who give Urdu as their mother tongue. Hence, they are also referred to as the 'Urdu people'. (Hereafter, the term is used throughout in this wider sense, and not for the people from Bihar only.)

These people, migrating from India in large or small groups during the Partition riots and the subsequent years, built their settlements in many towns and cities of what was then East Pakistan, especially in the north-western part of it, nearest to India proper. Apart from being more intelligent and hard-working than the local people, they were also the favourites of the Pakistani rulers, because in the language controversy which erupted almost with the inception of Pakistan, their loyalties and sympathies remained naturally with the West Pakistanis as opposed to the 'Bengalis'. As a reward for this support, they were accorded far greater opportunities for economic progress and prosperity than were the local people. Thus, during the 24 years of Pakistani rule, a fairly numerous class of successful entrepreneurs emerged from among the Biharis. This class is now lying almost prostrate in Bangladesh. And along with it, lakhs of common people—shopkeepers and middle class employees—have also lost their means of livelihood. Today in Bangladesh, to be a Bihari is the worst crime. And what is still more tragic is that the Biharis themselves have been largely responsible for bringing about this situation.

In numerous little towns and scattered places, where these people had settled in small numbers, there is no trace of them today. It is an established fact that during the first phase of the active freedom struggle in Bangladesh—in the months of March, April and May 1971—when as a result of the revolt of the Bangla Army Regiments and the Police, almost the entire country had slipped out of Pakistani control temporarily, Biharis were killed and their properties looted in scores of places, especially in the border areas. Later, beginning from June 1971 onwards, when the Pakistani military succeeded in re-establishing its hold, the stream of blood started to flow in the opposite direction. The Biharis and the military now killed as many Bangla nationalists as they could lay their hands on. Thus, it was in every sense of the term a civil war, only fought in two phases, in which both sides perpetrated the most inhuman atrocities on one another, killing and maiming like demented savages on the rampage.

There is no point today in computing and comparing the death rolls, for, in the eyes of the world, both the 'Banglas' and the 'Biharis' stand guilty of unsurpassed brutality against fellow beings. What matters and has to be attended to immediately is that among both the communities today, lakhs of people are naked, hungry and jobless, thousands of women helpless without husbands, and numberless children orphaned. The only difference is that the plight of the 'Bengali' is thinly seen, being spread over some 7½ crore people over a vast area, while that of the Bihari lies thick in a number of small concentrations, crushing the life out of nearly half of them. In any case, those who come here from outside with an open mind and look at the problem from an impartial but sympathetic standpoint, don't have to look long to see that what has happened in Bangladesh is only a man-made human tragedy as must inevitably follow every war or civil war. In itself, war is tragic. But still more tragic are the consequences that flow from it.

Today, in Dacca proper, the situation is still so abnormal as to deter an easily recognisable Bihari from walking alone on a lonely road. Even the short-statured and dark-skinned among them, who resemble the 'Bengalis', and so do move about with a little less anxiety, avoid speaking the Urdu language as if it were poison. It really stands them in good stead today that they were sociable enough during the many years of their domicile here to pick up and be able to speak the local dialect fairly well. It helps them to carry on their avocations with some safety, while it also protects them from hostile attention from the Banglas.

To speak Urdu in public was almost an invitation for death immediately after Independence. Even today, while it will not lead to anything so serious, it may still attract a sudden jerk or push from behind from some Bangla patriot. As the writer, being intent on making observations, made it a point to speak only in Urdu with his Bihari friends in Dacca almost everywhere, despite their repeated warning about the risk involved, he had to suffer for his folly a few 'back-shakes' in crowded bazars!

In new Dacca, around Motijheel Commercial area, some Bihari firms have now reopened, or, to put it more correctly, new businesses have been launched in place of the older, plundered ones. But their number can be counted on finger tips. The few businessmen and their staff who work in these firms with stoic courage can still be seen handling their papers or lifting the receiver with trembling hands. And this condition obtains even when these businessmen, by paying heavy donations, have gained the support and protection of the ruling Awami League. They must also close down by 4 P.M., for the Awami League, apparently, cannot guarantee protection to them after this hour.

The former owners of most Bihari shops and businesses in the city are untraceable, and very few well-known Biharis now live in their accustomed places. Unclaimed Bihari shops and businesses, which somehow still exist intact, are being run under Government control, with appropriate sign-

boards announcing the fact. The thousands of
'vacant' houses, the illegal occupation of which is
described in some previous chapter, belong mostly
to Biharis and West Pakistanis, and also to those
who took refuge in India. Some of the last group
are still waiting for their properties to be restored,
and many of them have not returned at all.

Most of the Biharis in Dacca are still confined
to the two colonies which made headlines after the
14-day war in December 1971. These are Mohammedpur and Mirpur, both situated in the north-
western corner of the western half of new Dacca.
Built more or less on the same lines as the dozens
of Punjabi colonies in Delhi, both were formerly
pure Bihari colonies. And just as the Punjabi
refugees in Delhi later transformed their tiny
quarters into fine houses by investing their own
hard-earned money on them, so did most of the
Bihari colonists in Mohammedpur and other towns.
But today it is not the Biharis but the Bangla
people who live in many of these fine houses, because the owners have either disappeared or are
presumed dead. Even some of those who are alive
and still here find it safer to live not in their houses
but in the relief camps that have been set up in
these colonies since after the December war. I
had an opportunity of visiting one of them, the
Mohammedpur Camp, where I took down the statements of the local Bihari leaders. The visit was
a most heart-rending and unforgettably tragic
experience.

But before a description of this inhuman camp
is attempted, it is necessary to grasp the viewpoint

of the Biharis themselves with regard to the causes of their present misfortune. For, without this fundamental understanding, much of what the Bihari representatives are going to tell us, will remain unintelligible. Conversations with various Bihari businessmen and intellectuals in Dacca had revealed three different viewpoints which the Biharis generally adopt in reviewing the present conditions and the events preceding them. The common element in all three will become evident to the reader, with no necessity for the writer to point it out. It must, however, be stated that this common element is indeed the root cause of both their miserable downfall and their present excruciating suffering.

The first point of view asserts that the main charge against the Biharis—that of having been anti-Bangladesh—is wrong and unfounded. As evidence, the results of the 1970 elections in certain constituencies, said to be the only ones with Bihari majorities, are cited; in these, Bangla candidates of the Awami League won as against Bihari candidates of the communal parties. On enquiry in official circles, however, it turns out that none of these constituencies have Bihari majorities; they are all Bangla majority constituencies. Thus, there is no evidence to show that the Biharis as a whole did not oppose Bangladesh, rather there is much evidence to prove the contrary. In fact, if human nature and logic are any guide, the Biharis ought to have opposed Bangladesh tooth and nail, and that was exactly what they did. To be fair to them, however, it has to be admitted that, under the circumstances obtaining then, there was nothing immoral or unpatriotic in their conduct. As

Pakistanis with a vested interest in the unity of
Pakistan, they were duty-bound to try to keep the
two parts of Pakistan together if they could. That
the six-point programme of the Awami League,
then the main issue for something like a plebiscite,
contained the germs of an eventual break-up, could
hardly be denied by any man in his senses. So,
the Biharis had every reason, democratically
speaking, to oppose the establishment of a semi-
independent Bangladesh,as long as it did not materialise. Their stand today should, therefore, take the
form not of defending past actions but of accepting
defeat with grace and offering to fall in line, subject
to acceptance.

According to this first viewpoint, the reason
why the Banglas became such deadly enemies of
the Biharis is set down as economic—and to that
extent the reasoning is correct. It is true that the
comparatively greater prosperity of a class among
them, and also their general success in capturing a
disproportionately larger share of the jobs and
businesses, did lead to heart-burning among the
Banglas, and to all the poison that inevitably flowed
from it. Without a doubt, this economic disparity
worked as the main element in fanning the fires of
Bangla nationalism. But the Biharis must also
concede that their own undoubted talents were not
the only decisive factor in the game; the partiality
and patronage of the Pakistani rulers, however
natural and understandable, had also played a big
hand in bringing about the disastrous situation.

The second viewpoint presented is what might
be called 'purely Islamic'. It holds that there

was, in fact, neither any mass movement for greater rights in Bangladesh, nor any opposition on the part of the Biharis to whatever there was, nor indeed any particular hatred for the Biharis among the Banglas ! All that happened was that "India, the sworn enemy of Pakistan, having bought up some Bangla leaders with its money and greater cunning-ness, incited a mock rebellion in Bangladesh with the help of these stooges, and then by hatching up an international conspiracy with three great powers——the USA, the USSR, and the UK—it broke Pakistan into two by sheer brute force !" The final exact words of the intellectual, a graduate of Allahabad University, who represented this very common viewpoint, were as follows: "Pakistan was an absolutely sound, healthy and viable organism; there was nothing wrong either in its constitution or in its conduct. But when four powers, acting in concert, used far superior force to tear it asunder, how could Pakistan successfully resist such over-whelming odds, especially when her only ally, China, too would not come to her aid for fear of Russia!"

Having patiently heard out this theory (there are many in India who also support it), I felt like asking the gentleman, 'Well, friend, let's go to the stairs of Masjid Bait-ul-Mukarram nearby, and there, in the name of God, you explain this theory in 'the national language of Pakistan' to those thousands of 'good Pakistanis' who throng this revered place all day long. May God crown your effort with success.' But to say such a thing would have meant inflicting another wound on an already bleeding heart. So I said only this: "Dear friend, no country is free from foreign agents and mercenary stooges. But such people do not lead popular movements, nor do they fight elections and capture Parliaments. Indeed, if by chance or mistake, they ever happen to hold elections, they themselves are washed away in the resulting tidal wave, like poor Yahya. And if your theory is that this entire new nation has mortgaged its freedom to India or to the other powers you mention, then, where is the question of any treason ? A people are sovereign; they can decide even to cease to be ! But, of course, you can always express an opinion."

The third viewpoint seeks to assert that the Biharis were neutral, but they wished justice had been done to East Pakistan. It is admitted that the eastern wing was subjected to continuous and grave injustices. But for that the military rulers in Islamabad were responsible, not the poor Biharis here. The Biharis suffered because they had ties of blood and language with the West Pakistanis; and the Banglas had only them within reach to wreak vengeance on when they were oppressed. What they could not do to the oppressing but powerful Pak military, they did to the neutral and weak Biharis by proxy.

There is no doubt an element of truth in all this. But even this nicely-balanced and rational viewpoint suffers from a serious fallacy. If justice was to be done to East Pakistan in accordance with the universally accepted principles of the present-day world, then East Pakistan should have had the status usurped by West Pakistan. In other words, everything from the national capital to larger

investments should have been located in this wing.
But then the result would have been an almost
immediate rebellion in the West and its separation
from Pakistan within a few years instead of the
24 years taken by the East. And, subsequently,
the remaining Westerners would, in any case, have
been driven out of the residual 'Pakistan' in the
East just as they have been in actual fact. So,
by working on the principle of justice, all of Pakistan
would have vanished long ago, whereas by adopting
the principle of injustice, at least a country by the
name of Pakistan still exists on the map of the world !

*   *   *   *

It was in the company of my Bihari friends in
Dacca that I visited the Mohammedpur Relief Camp.
(These friends were former Urdu journalists from
Calcutta, and had been my colleagues in the fifties.)
As stated above, the other colony, Mirpur, too has
a camp like this, and in the two of them some three
lakh people are presently hovering between life and
death. Of course, these are not the only relief
camps for Biharis in Bangladesh today; such camps
exist in almost a dozen places all over the country
—at Saidpur, Rangpur, Bogra, Jessore, Khulna,
Chittagong, Mymensingh, Rajshai, Ishardhi, Admaji
Nagar, etc. According to the Bangladesh Red Cross,
a total of some 7½ lakh Biharis have been given
shelter in these camps—which is another way of
saying that exactly half of the known Bihari population in Bangladesh (15 lakhs) are at present
living in camps on charity.

Mohammedpur Relief Camp is spread out on a
large open piece of land in the centre of the colony.

Beginning with the December war, it started taking
shape here, gradually spreading all over like some
slow, creeping thing of horror, found only in fiction
of that name. The camp is composed of more
than two hundred huge sheds made of mat and
bamboo. A road runs through the middle, dividing
the camp in two halves. The sheds of only one half
have tin roofs, while those of the other have mat
for roofs too. The floor everywhere is just plain,
raw earth. As such, one can well imagine the plight
of the afflicted humanity under these sheds, particularly under mat roofs, during the terrific monsoons
which descend on these parts for four months in the
year. Even without rain, mud, silt and over-
flowing stinking drains abound everywhere. Heaps
of garbage and excreta mark the inner lanes. The
stench is unbearable.

Every shed is partitioned by mat-screens into
some 50 or so small boxes or cells, the smallest
being only 10′×5′. In each such cell, a family
of five to ten persons has been stuffed in like some
inert material. Thus inserted, they stay there,
not even like vermin because vermin move; they
just stay there—motionless, expressionless, lifeless.
Looking at them in their mat-cells, one can scarcely
believe that these lumps of bone and skin can be
living human beings. They all appear to be dead.

Apart from those in the cells, the camp area as
a whole is also seething with naked, starving, disease-
ridden and blank-eyed humanity—men, women and
children—all seemingly locked in a life-and-death
struggle. Within minutes, the outside visitor starts
feeling suffocated, and a strange dread and dis-

belief descend on him: 'Can man live like this ?
Is all this possible ?'

Mohammedpur camp, at the time of the visit,
had 18,260 families or more than 1,46,000 people
on its rolls. Thousands of these people were well-
to-do till yesterday. Some were successful businessmen or executives in private concerns, others were
employees of the Railway and P & T Departments—
Government servants who had opted from India
in 1947 to serve Pakistan, or may be the employed
sons and nephews of those who opted. But few
of them can report for duty today for fear of their
lives. Thousands have been discharged from service
on the ground of 'long absence without leave'.
But their salaries and funds have not yet been paid.
Bank accounts too have been difficult to operate;
in any case, most are already exhausted. Many
persons rejoined duty on the strength of 'clearance
chits' given by Awami League M.P.'s. But they did
not return; even their bodies remained untraced.

Thus, thousands of these Government servants
and a larger number of petty businessmen and
workmen have been reduced to the same state of
destitution which is the normal lot of the majority
of the camp-dwellers. And like the latter, they
too now live entirely under the flimsy shelter of the
camp and on the doubtful charity of the world.
To what a state of social and moral degradation
this must have brought them, can easily be imagined.

The camp formerly was run under the direct
care of the International Red Cross, but for some
months now the Bangladesh Red Cross has taken

over. On its behalf, a Central Relief Organisation and a Managing Committee composed of local Bihari representatives look after the day-to-day affairs of the camp. The Bangladesh Red Cross is committed only to supplying 40 tonnes of wheat grain every day for the inmates, not a thing beyond that, although no less then 30 items of relief are recognised internationally. Even these 40 tonnes of grain are not supplied on a regular basis; both the quantity and the number of days never exceed 20 in a month. Thus, one can easily calculate the actual amount of daily ration that is distributed against the fixed quota of six chhattaks (less than a pound) per capita per diem. Naturally, many have to starve for days on end. As to what becomes of the nearly half of the total grain issued from Government godowns, can be known only to the Government. This observer felt that large-scale pilferage, black-marketing and other forms of corruption were resorted to by some in the camp management itself.

This very quota of six chattaks of wheat grain per capita per diem is also extended to many other Biharis, who live in their own quarters in the colony. Being unemployed, they too have been put on relief. If by chance, these house-owning people get the full quota, they exist by eating half of it and sell the other half to meet their sundry needs. Some petty bazars have sprung up within the camp, and a number of grinding mills have been set up to turn the grain into atta. Thus, a most painful and degrading form of localised economic system, based only on the wheat grain flowing fitfully from international charity, has emerged here. This

by itself constitutes a revealing commentary on the
present life-pattern of the Bihari inmates of the
colony and the camp. And the same conditions
must hold true of every other Bihari relief camp in
Bangladesh today. What is worse is that no
Bangla leader, of the ruling party or the opposition,
ever takes the trouble to visit the camps, nor do the
Bangla people generally show any sympathy for the
unfortunate Biharis huddled in their midst.

The local Bihari representatives affirm that no
proper procedure has ever been adopted to ascertain
the wishes of the Biharis with regard to citizenship.
Beginning from August 1972, many kinds of forms
have been distributed, but in them the question
has never been formulated on a clear-cut basis.
Besides, thousands of forms have still to be collected.
Thus, according to these representatives, the official
claim that 2,60,000 people have opted for Pakistani
citizenship, is fictitious. This figure, they say, is
simply put down on paper with the sole object of
sending out so many unwanted Biharis to make
room for the Banglas who are awaiting repatriation
from Pakistan.

However, these representatives also admit that
only about 20% of the Biharis here have any relations in Pakistan, while the other 80% have all
their relations in India; and so naturally they look
more towards India today than towards Pakistan.
They divulged that many of them are secretly
slipping into India by spending money or otherwise,
and the Government of India have so far adhered
to a policy of looking the other way. The Biharis
desire that this policy of leniency and compassion

on the part of the Indian Government should
continue.

But they are also conscious of the many political
difficulties now being faced by both India and
Bangladesh internally. As a principle, however,
they suggest that if Mujib Government itself could
ensure their civic security here, and, in place of the
present attitude of vengeance and retribution, adopt
a policy of clemency and reconciliation, the Biharis
could still stand on their feet again. But, if that is
not possible for political reasons, then, the only
solution is agreement between the three countries
for exchange with Pakistan, with India's help in
the matter of transport.[1]   But to determine precisely
who among the Biharis really want to go, the
necessary survey should be conducted under international auspices as has been suggested by Prime
Minister Sheikh Mujib himself.   The Biharis regard
this proposal as a rational and reasonable one, and
wish that this be implemented as early as possible.
The result, they hope, would remove the ill-feeling
that the Banglas have towards the Biharis as well
as any illusions that Pakistan may be harbouring.

---

1.   Such an agreement has now been reached between India and
     Pakistan, and Dacca may also become a party to it formally in the
     near future when Pakistan recognises Bangladesh. This, it is hoped,
     will solve the two-way repatriation problem of the Banglas in
     Pakistan and some of the Biharis in Bangladesh, though not of all
     the $7\frac{1}{2}$ lakhs now in camps.

CHAPTER 10

The Hindus of Bangladesh

OF THE 7½ crore people of Bangladesh, some 13 per cent are Hindus. This adds up to quite an impressive figure. One would, therefore, expect this fact to be reflected in the make-up of the general public. But it is not. The Hindus in Bangladesh today are not seen in public as they were before 1947; now, one has to specially search for them amongst the people.

Looking at the faces of the thousands of passers-by in the streets, no one can say with any certainty as to who amongst them are Hindus, though, in actual fact, there must normally be hundreds of them. One soon learns that the Hindus here have long since given up almost all their distinguishing marks and symbols.

Many Muslims can be readily recognised as such, say, by the style of their beards. But the Hindus have no such visible mark of recognition. As recorded earlier, the three most common forms of male clothing here are the lungi-vest, the kurta-pyjama, and the pants-bush-shirt. These are common for both Muslims and Hindus. The women, if they are seen, are, of course, all drapped in saris. The traditional Hindu attire, consisting of dhoti, kurta, and chaddar is now almost extinct here. A Hindu scarcely ever comes out of his house or restricted area in this dress. Even in their own houses, they rarely don the dhoti. At my first host's in Dacca, I did not see anyone wearing it. It looks as if only some old people and a few high-brow traditionalists now come out attired in this fashion in public. But these persons too rarely go walking; they ride in carriages.

During my entire 16-day stay in Dacca, I noticed only one 'Hindu' in the street. He was a diminutive, emaciated, middle-aged person, clothed in a somewhat soiled dhoti and shirt, and was going along quietly with an open umbrella in his hand. Despite his inconspicuousness, he too was attracting the attention of passers-by. They would pause or turn their heads to cast an amused look at him, as if he were some rare animal. Oh yes, I remember: I saw another 'Hindu', in the ministerial office of Mr. Dhar. His simplicity and humility too was remarkable. He had a bundle of old, musty, dog-eared papers under his arm, and was requesting a meeting with the Minister. However, he was curtly put off for a week by the Private Secretary.

To 'see' the Hindus of Bangladesh under such conditions, therefore, I had to make some special efforts: I began with the Ram Krishan Math in Dacca. Situated at the junction of the old and the new city, in the area known as Tikatoli, it is a fairly spacious, well-maintained and clean spot. Next to the compound just inside the gate, is a nice little

flower garden, with a small Kali temple on one side
and some rooms and other quarters in front and
on the other side. The rooms are meant for the
Swamis of the mission and their guests, and the
quarters are presumably for the staff. In the front
compound also, there are some more quarters and a
school on one side and a dispensary on the other.
The school and the dispensary, apparently, cater to
the needs of the Muslim population of the neighbour-
hood.

Here, at the mission, by the grace of the Swamiji
in-charge, I had the opportunity of meeting some
Hindu representatives and acquainting myself with
their viewpoints. After that, I spent a whole day
going around the old city, looking for other Hindu
representatives. Passing through Tikatoli, Narinda,
Lukhkhi Bazar, Sankhari Bazar, Islampur Road,
down to Sadar Ghat (Steamer Station) on the Buri
Ganga river, and then back through Liaquat Avenue
and Nawabpur, I traversed the entire south-eastern
half of the old city. Nowhere did I see a single
'Hindu' in the street. The famous Hindu street,
Sankhari Bazar, I passed through twice. The
congested, old-style houses on either side of this
narrow street, said to have been set on fire by the
Pakistani Army, now bore little evidence of a fire,
though the houses themselves were in a state of
total decay. The street too didn't look very much
'Hindu'; there were not many Hindu sign-boards
on the shops below. The owners of these houses,
since their return from India, may have reoccupied
the disintegrating apartments above. But I saw
no human face peeping out of any window or
verandah.

The old city, at many places, looks very much like the Matia Mahal bazar of old Delhi. The narrow streets have the same din and bustle, the same crowding, the insanitation, the ever-jammed traffic of cycle-rickshaws and other slow-moving vehicles, old-style shops with tarpaulin awnnings, dirty restaurants and stinking tea-stalls, with more or less the same kind of clientele as can be observed any day in the typical old Delhi street. The only difference is in the script used on the signboards. However, mosques seem to be an exception to the general squalor in old Dacca. At every turn, there is a mosque, and most are well-designed and well-built, with high quality stone-lining and other embellishments. It is said that in no other city of the world are there as many mosques as there are in Dacca.

The Hindu representatives I met at the mission, and later in their homes and offices did not want their names published. So, they have to remain anonymous for the time being. But what they told me in great detail did not hold out a very promising and hopeful future for the Hindus here, although Mr. Manoranjan Dhar, the Minister, had expressed the opposite view. For an under-standing of this other side of the story, a rapid review of this country's history over the past 25 years is necessary.

The condition to which the Hindus of Bangladesh have been reduced is a result of the 24 years of Pakistani rule; and the upheaval of the past two years has not brought about any significant change in this condition, except that the individual Hindu's sense of personal security has somewhat improved. On the political plane, the only important development so far has been that just as in India some Muslim party members are elevated to ministerships to hoodwink the Muslims, so has Sheikh Saheb taken in two Hindus as his trusted colleagues. But in this country Hindu ministers have functioned even under the Pakistani regime; so, by itself, the inclusion of Mr. Majumdar and Mr. Dhar in the present cabinet is no great event for the Hindus.

The fundamental stand of the Hindus here is that in 1947, Bengal was partitioned against their wishes and without their consent. But since, due to the communal set-up of the province, the Hindu (Congress) members were predominantly from the western districts and those from the east were less in number, and the decision on partition was to be taken by the Hindu and the Muslim members separately, the Hindus from the west succeeded easily in getting the decision adopted by a majority. Of course, some deserters from the east also supported the decision. But most of the eastern members did not, or might have done so only under duress. In any case, even those who openly sided with the west, later took the first opportunity to run away from here; and one of those renegades was made the first Chief Minister of West Bengal after Independence. Thus, according to the Hindu representatives whom I am reporting here in more or less their words, the Hindus of West Bengal, for their own selfish interests, sacrificed the Hindus of East Bengal.

Subsequently, an eight-man delegation with

such leading lights as N. C. Chatterjee, Shyama Prasad Mukherjee, Keshab Banerjee and Meghnad Saha met with Jawaharlal Nehru at Delhi, and protested to him against the injustice then being done to the East Bengali Hindus. But Nehru argued with them that had Bengal not been partitioned, the whole of it would have gone to Pakistan. "So, by partitioning it, we have saved a part of it and Calcutta for India," he said. The second point he put forward was that even this partition in its then absolute form would prove to be a temporary one. His words as quoted were as follows: "East Pakistan will not last even for two years. West Pakistan may succeed as a separate country, but not the Eastern wing. The East will only be exploited by the West, till it will be forced to snap its connections with the latter and establish friendly relations with India. So, East Bengal will not remain an enemy country for ever; it will be a friendly one. Your inconvenience is, therefore, a matter of a few years. . . ."

Even then, the delegation pointed out the many difficulties that the Hindus were going to face in East Pakistan, and insisted on a mass exodus. Thereupon, Nehru took up a map and started arguing again: "This East Pakistan, as you can see, is surrounded on all sides by India. If anything happens to you there, India can always come to your aid. You are not so far-removed from the power centres of India as to have no recourse but to follow the example of the West Pakistani Hindus and Sikhs. Even so, if you cannot really stay on in East Pakistan, you can always come out. India's doors are always open to you. But you must not

come at this moment, because with the rehabilitation of the Western refugees taking up all our
resources, it would not be possible for us to rehabilitate another 1½ crore people right now." In short,
the delegation was persuaded to accept Nehru's
reasoning; and thus the bulk of the Hindus of East
Bengal were induced to stay on where they were.

After the 1950 riots, another delegation went
to Calcutta, and had long discussions with the then
Minister of Rehabilitation, Mr. Mehr Chand Khanna,
at N. C. Chatterjee's house. But Khanna, or rather
the Government of India, would on no account
agree to treat the refugees from East Pakistan on
a par with those from West Pakistan. Thus, the
main reason for the Hindus to stay on here was the
absence of a guarantee of their rehabilitation in
India. Had they been given the same right to
compensation as was extended to the evacuees
from the West, no Hindu would perhaps have
remained in East Pakistan.

While living here, the Hindus had a number of
problems on their hands. The first was, of course,
the so-called communal riots which occurred every
now and then, and in which the so-called 'Bihari'
refugees from India generally had the major hand.
For the resettlement of these refugees, houses, shops,
lands, and businesses were needed, and these
things in 'Islamic Pakistan' could be snatched only
from the Hindus. So, riots were engineered, so
that the plundered and terror-stricken Hindus would
leave their homes and shift to India. In the riots,
which usually took the form of looting, burning,
and stabbing, the attitude of the Pakistani adminis-

tration was always unsympathetic towards the afflicted minority. In fact, many of the riots were actually the making of the Authorities themselves.

In addition to this almost constant threat to life and property, another problem the Hindus had to face concerned their honour. Their self-respect too was threatened all the time. One form of this threat was the practice of abducting any Hindu girl found unprotected and forcibly marrying her to a Muslim. Even if some of these cases eventually went to court, the magistrates, under the influence of the peculiar ideology of Pakistan, would attach little importance to them. On the contrary, they would deliver a lecture to the complainant on how mutual feelings of love and affection were going to be strengthened and a united Pakistani nation brought into being by such marriages of Hindu girls among Muslims. Even if the idea was rationally appealing, in the given context of the religion-oriented societies in these parts, such marriages (not to speak of forced ones) could lead, not to the strengthening of love and affection but only to more hatred and bloodshed.

A gentleman related an interesting story about these marriages. After an abducted girl had been recovered, the senior begum of the judge hearing the case came to the girl's parents and told them that since the girl had already fallen in their estimation and was of no further use to them, they had better hand her over to her, because her own husband, the Judge Saheb, was interested in marrying her ! Fortunately, this particular girl was saved from this marriage, and was sent to India with her parents.

More than abduction and forcible marriages, what really worried parents of girls was another kind of harassment which on the face of it looked 'very honourable'. The method was simply to address a letter of proposal to the father of any Hindu girl who might have struck the eye of the proposer. These letters very often carried the full addresses of the would-be bridegrooms. But when the harassed fathers, feeling very much slighted, went to seek police aid against the culprits, they were asked, according to the same Pakistani ideology, as to 'what was wrong in the honourable proposal ! At the most, they could say that the proposal was not acceptable to them. But what could the police do in such matters ! Surely, to ask for the hand of a girl was not a crime !' It is not difficult to see that the main object of all these activities was not to bring into existence any united Pakistani nation, but simply to harass the Hindus to the point of desperation, so that they were forced to quit Pakistan.

The fourth misfortune that visited the Hindus arose out of the attachment of their properties and businesses. Job opportunities for the Hindus, both in Government and private services, had ceased almost from the day Pakistan came into being. The bigger zamindaris under the Permanent Settlement had also broken up automatically after the voluntary exit of the raja-zamindars. Hence, when the East Pakistan Abolition of Zamindari Act, 1952, came into force, the Government experienced little difficulty in taking over the estates without compensation and parcelling them out

among the cultivators. Thus, all that remained
with the Hindus was some self-cultivated land,
houses, and a few businesses. But since the owners
of these properties were always moving both ways
across the border, the Government, taking advantage
of some technicality, would suddenly move its
Custodian to step in. And then, for years on end,
cases would drag on in the courts, resulting in much
suffering and expense for the Hindus.

Besides private properties, trusts and religious
endowments too were very often taken over. Trusts
worth crores thus went under Government control
or management in East Pakistan. Even those
which somehow escaped the Pakistani drag-net
were forced to have Government nominees on their
managing committees; the Deputy Collector or the
SDO was appointed compulsory chairman of such
Committees. In short, as the Hindu representatives
put it, 'while the policy of the Pakistan Government
 was aimed at gradually squeeing out the Hindus
from its domain, that of the Indian Government
was dead set against allowing the Hindus to come
out.'

To the question as to how did the Hindus survive such grim conditions, the reply was that the
Hindus in East Pakistan had adopted a number
of techniques for their protection. The first among
these was that if, say, they received a beating in
Dacca, they would shift to some village in the interior
where they had relatives. People in the villages
who were familiar with them and spoke the same
language were not given to starting riots like the
Bihari refugees and their collaborators among the

local hooligans in the cities. Even so, if it became difficult to hold on to the village, they would move further away, towards India. After all, it was India that lay all around. So, as a final resort, many people would just move out of the country as refugees, even though it meant losing all their possessions. Thus, one way of saving their lives was in not confronting or resisting the aggressors. Even where forcible occupation of land or property was involved, and the Hindu owners succeeded in getting court orders in their favour, they would not take steps to have those orders executed. Similarly, in abduction cases involving girls, many people would just reconcile themselves to the outrage and do nothing. This policy of persistent non-resistance or non-violence, which is the only policy feasible for the weaker side, helped demoralise the rioters and brought the Hindus the support and sympathy of kindly people from among the majority community.

The second technique of self-defence was, of course, conversion. No doubt, this was resorted to only by the lower-caste, illiterate people. Their conversion too was only in name, and it made little difference either to themselves or to the Hindu society as a whole. The converted remained in the same lowly occupation and category as before. But the Pakistani rulers felt highly pleased at the nominal increase in the number of Muslims in their domain. In any case, conversion did offer an easy way out for many poor and helpless people.

The third method lay in bringing about a fundamental change in regard to dress, make-up, and outer mode of living. Almost all Hindus in the cities gave up their traditional form of dress and took to the lungi and the kurta-pyjama like the majority community. Previously, the Hindus here wore the lungi only in the house and went out in public in dhoti-kurta. The old practices of putting a tilak on the forehead or of having other distinguishing marks or symbols on the body publicly were also given up. As for women, they hardly ever came out of their houses in Pakistani times. In fact, Hindu women had taken to the veil while many of their Muslim sisters were discarding it. If they had to go anywhere, they would go only in closed carriages.

Likewise, the usual practice of greeting people with namaskar, etc., was given up insofar as others were concerned. In its place, the manners of Adab and Salam were adopted. During certain very dark periods, even Arabic names started appearing among the Hindus along with Sanskrit names. Some exceptionally faint-hearted people even had the 'khatna' performed on them, 'for the only sure proof of innocence that could save a man from being knifed was a private part, well circumcised !' Conversions too were confined only to this surgery.

But the most effective and successful technique was that of not competing with or confronting the majority community in the political and economic fields. The Hindus here had firmly made up their mind from the very first day that leadership and rulership of this country was not going to be any of their business. Very few Hindus would, therefore, take any active interest in politics. Even in civic affairs, their participation was nominal and subdued. Only some traditional leaders at the top would make deals with the rulers in the name of the community, though in actual practice the community got little benefit from them.

In their businesses and professions too, the Hindus maintained a low profile. In most cases, they would not conduct their affairs on their own; they would either go in for 'benami' business, or straightaway take partners from among their co-professionals in the majority community. In fact, apart from security, which such partnerships ensured, no useful dealings with the Government were possible without them.

In this connection, an advocate related an episode that occurred after the 1965 war. At that time, many Hindu assets and concerns were being confiscated under Ayub's Enemy Property Ordinance. However, in the case of a certain jute mill, the respondents succeeded in getting a quash order from the High Court. But when a lawyers' delegation met President Ayub to have the decree executed, the latter told them plainly that 'however much they might dangle the law before him, he was not going to let the Hindus get away with it.' He said : "Gentlemen, I have many arms. Whatever you take back from my one hand, I will snatch it again with the other. And the reason thereof you may hear from my secretary."

During the talk, the delegation had advanced the argument that the Hindus of Pakistan were, after all, Pakistanis; and if India attacked Pakistan,

she was an enemy of all Pakistanis. Subsequently,
when the delegation met the secretary, they were
told by him that what the President meant was
that, according to his belief, 'Pakistani' stood only
for a Muslim, and that a Hindu could never be a
Pakistani. The Hindus were the enemy, and,
therefore, they could not enjoy the protection of
Pakistani laws. It was because of such factors that
the Hindus in East Pakistan thought it wiser to have
Muslim partners in business and to withdraw almost
completely from most other fields of activity.

This withdrawal of the Hindus from open
competition—which was partly under duress and
partly out of free choice—had the beneficial effect
of gradually convincing the majority community
that their real exploiters were not the hated Hindus,
but their own Pakistani co-religionists. And this
realisation on their part became the main driving
force which in due time replaced the older 'zamindar-
tenant conflict' of a communal nature with a new
conflict that was almost of the nature of a class-
war. It was this that eventually led to the establishment of Independent Bangladesh.

As is well-known, during the Pakistani crackdown in 1971, the bulk of the Hindus of East
Pakistan took refuge in India. The exodus was
also in accordance with the wishes of the Pakistani
rulers, who hoped that the evacuees would never
come back, so that their own problem of a 'Bengali'
majority in Pakistan would be solved for all time.
Besides, India would be faced with a serious crisis
in her Bengal and possibly further afield. On the
other hand, the Bangla nationalists too were of

the opinion that it would be better if, during the active phase of the struggle, the Hindu minority were not present, so that the Pakistani rulers would have little opportunity to thwart the movement by staging communal riots. On the third side of the triangle, India's national interest also demanded, besides the question of human compassion, that a limited but large enough number of refugees should cross over, so that she could have a handle to turn what was an internal matter of Pakistan into an international one. Thus, the Hindus got 'aid' from all the three parties involved in the show-down; only the Hindus themselves were not involved. During the nine months of preparation for war, they lived in Indian camps in conditions of comparative ease and safety.

During those months of terror, the few Hindus left behind in the country used to have a most extraoidinary and, at the same time, a somewhat embarrassing experience. As the Pakistani action gained momentum and seemed to be succeeding all over the country, while India apparently showed no signs of making a decisive counter-move, Bangla nationalists would come to the few Hindus and bemoan: "You people are sitting there comfortably in Indian camps, and we are dying here everyday in our thousands. How long would your India be sitting like this with folded hands? Why doesn't she attack? It seems your India is betraying us!" So, that was the position of the Hindus in the eyes of the majority community here.

How are they faring now, since their return to Independent Bangladesh? To this the representatives gave diverse replies, the gist of which can be set down somewhat as follows: No doubt, the sense of personal security has improved; to deny that would be to do injustice to the new regime. But, at the same time, in view of the tremendous success achieved by Sheikh Mujib and his Awami League, and especially because of India's decisive role in bringing about the independence of Bangladesh, the Hindus here have become unusually hopeful that many of their long-standing grievances will now be redressed. Ordinarily, they would not have set much hope by any Government in this country; but after such revolutionary changes in the entire set-up, it is but natural that they should have hopes of some betterment in their conditions.

As long as the Indian Army stayed here, the general treatment accorded to the Hindus was decidedly better. At that time, the Hindus were not very numerous, though. But since the completion of the 'operation return' and the withdrawal of the Indian Army, even the general treatment seems to have become somewhat harder and colder. Such, at least, is the feeling among the Hindus. They attribute it to a possible fear or misconception among the Muslims that since Bangladesh has come into being through India's decisive action, the Hindus here might now try to sit on their heads again like in older times; they should, therefore, be kept in their places by tighter control and harder treatment.

In any case, it is true that the Hindus here who, under the Pakistani regime did not even expect human treatment, let alone justice, have now started expecting an almost magical reversal in their position under Sheikh Mujib. For example, they now naturally desire that the recruitment of Hindu youth to Government and semi-Government services, which was in total abeyance throughout the Pakistani period, should be reviewed and re-vived. Similarly, they draw attention to the many office regulations and circulars, etc., still in force, which enjoin discrimination against the Hindus; these too, they say, should be reviewed. During Pakistani times, the Hindus were required to take official permission before employing anybody even in their own businesses. Many such restrictions on the Hindus still continue. The Hindus desire that all this legacy of the past should now be done away with. (These Hindus had something more to say on this aspect in another context which will follow—Author). Thus, the first problem the Hindus want to be taken up relates to their employment and business.

The second problem is related to education and text books. Under the Pakistani regime, all educa-tion in this country was turned into a one-sided affair, in line with the ideology of the rulers, as though none but Muslims lived in Pakistan. All text books, save those of pure technology, were based on Islamic values. The same books, however, are still being used in Bangladesh. The only difference so far brought about is that wherever the word 'Pakistan' occurs, 'Bangladesh' has been super-imposed, or the books themselves have been reprinted after making this change in the text,

These books suffer from the defect that while they are quite suitable for a cent per cent Muslim society, they are not so for a mixed one. The lessons that occur in books on language, sociology, history, etc., for example, contain only such ideas as have relevance to Muslims alone. For instance, some of the themes of these lessons are 'the virtues of monotheism, the sinfulness of idolatry, the deliciousness of beef', etc. Similarly, there are lessons on customs, family relations, festivals, etc., but the subject-matter everywhere concerns only the Muslims. Among the great men, the bene-factors of humanity, heroes, brave boys, brave women, and the like, there is not a single non-Muslim name. All the conquerors, explorers, scientists, inventors, historians, and scholars seem to have been only Muslims. Every quotation or moral maxim is from Islamic books. History too seems to be a chronicle only of Islamic conquests. Thus, by reading these books, a non-Muslim child would learn nothing about himself, while a Muslim child would acquire only hatred and contempt for the non-Muslims. No doubt, all this is a legacy of the past, but its continuance in today's secular Bangladesh is certainly an anachronism; and the Hindus now feel very strongly about it. Perhaps, the official excuse would be that it is not possible to change overnight what has been in force for 25 years. On the writer's pointing this out, it was enquired sarcastically as to 'how many days were there in a Mujib night ?'

The third problem revolves round the question of restoring the trust properties of temples, etc., attached in Pakistani times, and the repair and re-building of some of the temples damaged or totally destroyed by the Pakistani Army. The famous Kali Bari temple in Ramna Maidan (now Suhrawardy Uddayan), the Anand Mai Bari nearby, the Luxmi Narain temple in Lakhkhi Bazar, the Shiv Bari temple in Tanti Bazar, Madhavpuri Math, and several other major and minor temples were either razed to the ground or greatly damaged by the Pakistani Army during the crackdown. Some people said that only Dhakeshwari temple and the Ram Krishan Math were the two important places which survived the Pakistani onslaught. Even in the Math, the idol had to be re-installed by the Swamis, as the Army had smashed the older one. Several temples were in unauthorised occupation when the Hindus returned, and special efforts had to be made to get them vacated. For instance, the Luxmi Narain temple in Nawabpur was vacated only on the personal intervention of Sheikh Mujib. The squatters were mostly communal goondas who had overnight become patriots by donning the Awami League garb. This writer himself, during his tour of the old city, saw several temples which had signs of damage inside and locks on the doors.

Sheikh Mujib does try to console and cheer up the Hindus in this regard. But he too has yet to muster enough courage to permit the re-building of the temples that are no more. In regard to Ramna Kali Bari temple, which has completely vanished (this was checked and confirmed by the writer personally), a Hindu delegation is said to have met Sheikh Mujib some time after Independence. These days the democratic Sheikh is very particular in showing regard to old Hindu leaders. He would greet them in the traditional Bengali style, embrace them, and then sit with them to bemoan the present unfavourable conditions. But in the matter of permitting the reconstruction of this particular temple, his excuse was that people presently were suffering from want of food and shelter; the threat of famine and large-scale starvation was hovering overhead. In such grim circumstances, the rebuilding of the temple so soon after Independence would only have an adverse effect on the people. One informant quoted Sheikh Mujib as having said something like this to the delegation: "Gentlemen, right now, Banga Bandhu is only an Indian agent! But if you start rebuilding the temple in haste, he shall become a Hindu agent too! So, please have some patience; the time for rebuilding the temple will also come."

The excuse was reasonable. But the Hindus say that the argument of famine and starvation does not seem to hold good for those dozens of mosques which are presently under construction all over the country. At Sadar Ghat in Dacca alone, four new mosques have appeared after Independence, whereas previously there was none at this spot. Similarly, on either side of the Ramna Maidan, the construction of two magnificent new mosques is going apace, despite serious shortages of all kinds. This is the Hindu viewpoint. But the writer believes, and said so to the representatives, that they should appreciate the delicate position in which Sheikh Mujib finds himself today. At the moment, he needs not only the mosques that are already under construction but perhaps a few more! After all, our own Prime Minister, Indira Gandhi, on her visit to Andhra before the 1972 General Election, had to forget her claims of being a Vedanti Brahmavadi when she went to have darshan of Bhagwan Vanketeshwar at Tirupati! In a democratic polity, the sentiments of the predominant majority have got to be catered to!

At the moment, the Hindus in Bangladesh are facing two immediate problems. One is the question of the restoration of property to returnees from India, some of whom are still in the woods. And the other is that of the notices which are still being served on Hindu property-holders under the Enemy Property Act of 1965. The Hindus allege that many returnees were not reinstated in their properties due to various technical reasons, but mainly because of the affected properties being in the illegal occupation of so-called Awami League leaders themselves. In this connection, they name three top-ranking leaders of the ruling party and demand an open inquiry into their affairs. These leaders are Kurban Ali, Vice-President, Awami League; Shah Muazzam, Chief Whip, Awami League Parliamentary Party; and Sheikh Sahib's nephew, Sheikh Fazal-ul-Haq Moni, who is the proprietor of the Daily Banglar Bani and the Press, and chief of the Juba League, the youth wing of the ruling party.

In the countryside, another complication in regard to evacuee property has arisen because of the desperate action of many people in accepting

money from the locals in exchange for property
before crossing over to India; these people had
evidently thought that they would not be coming
back this time. On their return, however, there
was a spate of civil cases, and the Government had
to appoint special tribunals to deal with the sudden
rush of litigation. The trouble is that even if a
decree is obtained, it is not always possible to have
it executed. On the first day, the bailiff might go
along with the party, but from the next day onwards,
personal security of the claimant becomes a doubtful proposition. That is why many people, even
after obtaining court orders, do not proceed to have
them implemented.

The second problem is still more complicated
and perplexing. It is true that the major owners
of many large-sized Hindu properties are in India,
and those who are occupying or managing the
assets here are either co-sharers in Hindu joint
families or just relatives with no direct interest
in the property. When such people are served
with show-cause notices, the queer thing is not the
notices themselves but the law under which these
are issued. As stated, it is the Enemy Property
Act of 1965, promulgated by Ayub with a view to
depriving the Hindus of East Pakistan of most of
their assets. But the continuation of action under
that law even today certainly shows a most ridiculous state of affairs. The writer personally saw
many such notices, which had only 'Government of
the People's Republic of Bangladesh' at the top
instead of 'Government of Pakistan'; the rest of
the text—the name of the Department, the Law and
the language, etc.—was exactly as before.

The Bangladesh Government has taken the firm stand from its very inception that it is not a successor government of Pakistan but a revolutionary government, and, therefore, it does not accept responsibility for any part of the foreign debts of erstwhile Pakistan, nor does it intend to pay any compensation to the West Pakistani owners of industries that have been nationalised. On the other hand, it issues notices of resumption to its Hindu citizens on the ground that the real or major owners of their properties are citizens of 'an enemy country'. Thus, India, technically and legally, continues to be 'enemy' in Bangladesh— which means that Bangladesh Government is legally a successor to erstwhile East Pakistan Government.

The Hindus say that this double position of the Government of Bangladesh is not just ridiculous; it is diabolical. It can only mean that when this Government wants to deprive the Hindus of their properties, it assumes the role of a successor to Pakistan, but when it faces the prospect of having to share a part of Bhutto's headache, it unfurls the banner of revolution.

The Hindus say that whatever might be the legal position of these properties, the dictates of human compassion, and especially the revolutionary changes that have taken place, clearly point to the advisability of devising a human solution of this problem. The real owners or the major partners should be allowed, they say, to have the properties formally registered in the name of their co-sharers and relatives. This alone would save these people from turning into another caravan of

refugees, whose trek to India and likely impact on
conditions there would in all probability restart
that whole unfortunate process of a two-way traffic
from which the emergence of Bangladesh has at
long last held out some hope of a final riddance.

On enquiry in knowledgeable circles, the writer
was told that the use of Ayub's law in present-day
conditions was certainly an anomaly. But the notices
themselves were not wrong. Similar notices were
being issued in West Bengal to Muslim citizens,
who were in extra-legal occupation of properties
belonging to Bangladeshi citizens. However, a
bill would soon be brought in Parliament, which
would rectify the situation by properly designating
these properties as 'abandoned' rather than 'enemy'.
How the affected Hindus and Muslims on either
side of the border were going to be benefited by
this verbal change, did not become immediately
clear to the writer.

In regard to the future, these Hindu representatives did not appear to be very optimistic. One
view was that like Pakistan's, the Mujib Government's policy too was to ease out the Hindus in
gradual stages. It was argued that in Pakistan,
at least, 'these people' needed the Hindus to maintain their majority, but now, after liberation, even
that necessity was over. Now, if the Hindus are
still here, that is because of the need for India's
friendship. The day this need too is done away
with, the Hindus will find themselves on the road
to India. Only Sheikh Mujib, to some extent, can
resist this process, but he is surrounded by all kinds
of Pakistani agents, communal fanatics, and plain

ruffians. Most of the Awami League's membership
is composed of thugs, dacoits, and cut-throats, and
the poor Hindus are entirely at their mercy, etc.,
etc. . . .

During the course of this very interesting and
revealing conversation, the complaint which I had
vaguely encountered almost everywhere among the
Hindus, was formulated in explicit terms. It was
to the effect that India, which had done so much
for Bangladesh, had sacrificed thousands of her
best sons for its liberation, was even now helping it
with such open-hearted generosity, should have
failed or forgotten to secure a proper guarantee of
justice for the Hindus here from this Government.
This failure or deliberate policy of the Indian
Government is puzzling to the Hindus here. The
writer had to point out that for the Indian Government to raise the issue of the Hindus here with the
Mujib Government, besides being against the principle of secularism, would have been an unwarranted
interference in the internal affairs of a sovereign
country. At this, the particular informant lost
his temper and castigated the writer somewhat in
the following words : "Mister, you show me one
'affair' of Bangladesh in which you do not have a
hand. Its foreign policy is determined by you.
Its defence policy is dependent on your good will.
Its entire trade is linked up with yours. Its POW's
are being kept and fed by you. Its Biharis are
your concern. Its citizens in Pakistan are your
concern. But the only thing that is not your
concern is we, the Hindus here. We alone are an
internal affair of Bangladesh ! What hypocrisy !"

The confusion of ideas displayed by this gentleman hardly calls for any comment.

As against this blatantly communal viewpoint, a leading Congressite expressed the opinion, or rather confirmed the opinion briefed to the writer by Mr. Dhar, the Minister, that "local Hindu (Congress) leaders have always been held in high esteem by democratic circles among the majority community, so much so that during some of the darkest periods of repression by the military rulers, the Bangla nationalists have held their secret meetings under our auspices. We have helped them in every possible way. We have as much hand in bringing about the independence of Bangladesh as the other nationalist parties. We do not, therefore, see any reason for losing heart so soon and becoming despondent."

He further said : "The extent to which we and India are respected and honoured by the elite here can be judged from the fact that many top-ranking lawyers, barristers, professors and other scholars have sincerely confided to us in private conversation that 'they would have felt far more secure and satisfied if India had straightaway turned the province into a special state of hers by just adding a clause 371 to her Constitution. In that case, they could have drawn on the entire resources of India for the development of their country.' To this we generally give the reply that India is no fool to take over the problem of feeding and clothing another $7\frac{1}{2}$ crore people and at the same time losing their friendship on the political plane. India has already enough problems of her own."

This leading Congressman further expressed the opinion that Sheikh Mujib and his Awami League Government would do everything in their power to see that democracy and secularism succeed in Bangladesh. But if, through a combination of internal and external forces inimical to India-Bangladesh friendship and their machinations against secularism, this objective was not achieved, and the Hindus here continued to have the feeling of being second-class citizens, then, of course, there would be no way out for them but to shift gradually to India. And, in that case, Bangladesh would by itself become 'Muslim Bengal'.

CHAPTER 11

Muslim Bengal ?

OF THE MANY controversies that have arisen as a result of the emergence of Independent Bangladesh is one that relates to the new state's nationality. Does the word 'Bengali' as used in Bangladesh have the same connotation as it has in India ? And if it does, as is claimed (with only a minor difference) by the two opposition leaders of Bangladesh, Professor Muzaffar Ahmed and Maulana Bhashani, then, which 'Bengal' includes the other ? Does Bangladesh include our Bengal, as claimed by Bhashani, or our Bengal includes Bangladesh as it did till 1947 ? Either equation will have its own logical consequences.

This problem might appear somewhat bizzare and irrelevant to Indian citizens outside West Bengal. But in Bengal it is important. For, a sentimental current, like the Maha Bangal movement of Maulana Bhashani in Bangladesh, is running through our Bengal too—which seeks to emphasize that the Bengali-speaking people, whether of Bangladesh or of the Indian Union, constitute 'one nation', and that this 'nation', therefore, should have a unified state of its own.

No doubt, all this is still confined to theoretical hair-splitting, no practical method of translating the idea into reality being yet in sight. Even in theory, there is great divergence of opinion as to whether the hypothetical 'united state' should be formed by enlarging Bangladesh or by applying that body-building treatment to Indian Bengal! The psychological difference between the two concepts will become clear as we proceed with this inquiry.

Very few people outside Bengal seem to realise that those in India who call themselves 'Bengali' do not use this word in the same comprehensive sense as, say, 'Punjabi' or 'Rajasthani' is used. All persons who have Punjabi or a Rajasthani dialect as their mother tongue can rightly be called 'Punjabis' or 'Rajasthanis'. But all persons who have Bengali as their mother tongue are not necessarily 'Bengalis'—which only goes to prove that language alone does not connote the name of a people, though it is always an important element in determining it. In other words, while nobody can be 'Bengali' without having Bengali as his mother tongue, merely having the language would not necessarily entitle a person to be called 'Bengali'.

'Bengali', essentially, is a social and cultural concept. It originated some two centuries ago when under the British East India Company's rule, a high-caste Hindu landlord class was brought into existence in Bengal. This class, on the strength of its vast unearned income and unlimited leisure, came into contact with the modern civilization and education of Europe through the agency of the

then British rulers. The new social values and
cultural trends that arose out of that contact and
assimilation had their impact on the high-caste
Hindu middle-class, too, because of natural imitation
of the then standard-setting feudal aristocracy.
Thus, a 'modern', educated society of high-caste
Hindus gradually emerged in Bengal. It was the
first modern society in India of those days, and the
modernism that later spread to other parts of the
country with the expansion of British Imperial
power, invariably followed the pattern set by the
pioneering Bengali society.

The members of this society alone were known,
and are still known, as 'Bengalis', and they are
referred to in common parlance as 'the bhadraloks'
(the gentry). A distinguishing feature of this
society is the almost universal literacy, including
some knowledge of English, prevalent amongst
its members—men, women, young and old alike.
Another symbol is that almost every family forming
part of it possesses at least one common hereditary
house somewhere in Bengal, with some agricultural
lands, orchards, etc., attached to it. The lands,
generally, are given over to share-croppers to till.
Those owners who are forced by circumstances to
till their lands are rarely referred to as 'bhadraloks',
even though they are high-caste. No doubt, in
the present-day, fast-changing economic conditions,
the Bengali 'bhadraloks' are finding it increasingly
difficult to maintain their status symbols. Nevertheless, the structure of the society, its cultural values
and, above all, its mental make-up remain exactly
as of old, with hardly any perceptible change.

This Bengali 'bhadralok' society is composed mainly of three well-known high castes of Bengal, namely, the Brahmins, the Vaidyas, and the Kayasthas. The Vaidyas are a special caste of Bengali Hindus, and are generally regarded as 'half-Brahmins', being entitled to discharge the functions of priesthood. The Kayasthas, on the other hand, though technically Shudras in Bengal, have always been a prosperous and influential community because of their attachment to learning and government service through the ages. So, they are also counted among the bhadraloks. Some isolated members of other Shudra sub-castes may also be admitted to this exclusive society through their acquiring knowledge and wealth over a few generations. But the crucial point is that all these people must necessarily be Aryanised Hindus for being included in the Bengali 'bhadralok' class. In other words, no low-caste Animistic Hindu, Tribal or Musalman, or member of some other denomination, can ever be regarded 'Bengali', however naturally he may speak the language or whatever his social status or learning. What is still more significant is that none of these other people, who in the case of the low-caste Animistic Hindus constitute almost 90 per cent of the Hindu population of Bengal, have ever laid claim to being 'Bengalis'. At least, no Musalman, at any stage in the history of Bengal, has ever claimed to be a 'Bengali'.

There is a Bengali-speaking Muslim officer at our High Commission in Dacca—a person of extraordinary wit and humour. He is known to be given to chiding his intimate Bangla visitors with the query: 'I say, Brother, could you tell me since when the Muslims of Bengal have become 'Bengali'? In our times, we had only two categories of people here, besides the dumb millions called 'chhotolok' (low people). These were the Bengalis and the Muslims. But now we hear that the Muslims too are 'Bengali'! What is this ?'

Whatever the reaction of the Bangla friends might have been to this friendly teasing, we must really consider the joke a pointer to a serious question. It is indeed worth enquiring as to how and when the Muslims of Bengal, by progress or retrogression, changed from their familiar, historical nomenclature to that of 'Bengali'. When in 1947, they threw in their lot with Pakistan (in fact, theirs was the major hand in the creation of Pakistan), they had no perception whatever of their being 'Bengali'. Indeed, had they that perception, they would hardly have consented to the partitioning of the province. At that time, they were only Musalmans, trying to carve out a separate homeland of their own, where they would be free from exploitation by the Hindus and enter the paradise of Islamic justice and equality. But the moment this paradise came into being, they became conscious that they were Bengalis first and Musalmans only after that. How and why did this metamorphosis take place ?

It came about because of the idiotic decision of the Pakistani rulers to declare Urdu as the only national language of Pakistan. They took this decision without any thought or preparation, and even though some efforts to mitigate its adverse effects were made on paper in later years, the harm to the concept of Pakistan had already been done and could not be reversed. So long as Urdu was just a language—a well-formed and sweat-sounding, literary and religious language—it had the same appeal for the Muslims of Bengal as it continues to have till this day for all Muslims in the sub-continent, including those whose mother tongue is not Urdu. But to declare it the only official language of Pakistan meant that the very purpose for which the Muslim elite of Bengal had plumped for Mr. Jinnah's theory was going to be negated; that is, this class, already neglected and suppressed for nearly two centuries, was going to be in the same position in Pakistan too, with no decisive hand in the running of the administration of that country.

Naturally, therefore, the first protest against that ill-conceived decision came from the student community—the young boys and girls who aspired for a future in the expanding bureaucracy. For them, 'Urdu only' meant a permanent disability in competition with the Urdu-knowing West Pakistani candidates. They also saw that if they had Bengali, the West Pakistanis would suffer from a still greater disability. So, why not have Bengali—which in any case was the language of the majority in Pakistan—as the only or at least the main language of the country ? Thus, for the first time in history, the politically conscious Muslims in Bengal (now in East Pakistan) became aware of the tactical importance of their language in the power game. And now no argument of Islamic brotherhood could turn them back from using

this language as their main weapon for securing
political power in the land. The more the Pakistani
rulers, in their theocratic blindness, tried to wean
the East Pakistani Muslims away from Bengali,
the more firmly they (East Pakistanis) attached
themselves to it. In fact, it was like Freedom for
India's youngmen prior to 1947: the East Pakistani
youth too could now very well lay down their
lives for the preservation of this language. Since,
however, the Pakistani rulers were intoxicated with
theocratic notions, they first threatened and then
actually fought this 'weapon of language' with their
own 'language of weapons'. As a result, some
valuable young lives were lost.

Since that blood-smeared date of February 21,
1952, when students fell to police bullets in front
of Dacca's Medical college, right up to the revolutionary date of December 16, 1971, when the green
and red flag of Independent Bangladesh was hoisted
over Dacca's Government House, all that the bulk
of the people of East Pakistan went through, and
the numerous other racial, geographical, political,
economic and psychological factors that combined
to give them their sense of 'separate identity'—
all this, in its essence, constitutes their nationhood.
No recapitulation of that history of 25 years is
necessary here. Only this has to be borne in mind
that all this history has taken place within Pakistan
and in the context and colour of Pakistan. This
history is related to the old history of older Bengal
only insofar as its origin and continuity are
concerned, but certainly not in its final form and
content

Therefore, when Sheikh Mujib says that "Nationalism has many connotations and many definitions. Seers and scholars of the world have presented many a definition of the concept. So, if I do not put forward a new one, no harm would be done. I can say only this that I, who am a man of Bangladesh, am a nation. Call it my language, my education, my civilization, or my culture, but along with all these things, there is something else. And that is my experience. Without this experience, no nation can stand on its feet; nationalism itself cannot evolve in its being. Many are the nations in the world who, despite having diverse languages within them, are nations. On the other hand, there are countries which have the same language, the same religion, the same everything, yet they have not evolved into single nations. In short, nationalism depends solely on feeling and experience. Today, this 'Bengali' nation of ours has gained its Independence through a bloody struggle. The basis on which this struggle was waged, the basis on which this Independence has been won—of that I have a sense. That is why I say that I am 'Bengali'; my nationalism is 'Bengali'." (Speech in Bangladesh Parliament, November 4, 1972). . . . . .

He says something which is absolutely correct. But, at the same time, this much has to be added to his exposition that this experience of a struggle and of attainment of Freedom has not been the same for all the people of Bangladesh. Even among the Bengali-speaking people, we can very easily spot a whole community which can be excluded, with good reason, from the ambit of this experience.

In the preceding chapter, the summarised statements of some selected representatives of the Bangladeshi Hindu minority are recorded. More than their content, it is the style of their presentation and the psychology that motivates them which show that the Hindus of Bangladesh as a whole have little mental or emotional affiliation with the winning of independence by 'their country'. Some individuals here and there may have taken an active, physical part, both in the movement and the final struggle. But that too has been in the context not of Bangladeshi nationalism but of a greater nationalism, which in their view encompasses Bangladesh, but can also do without it.

As a community, therefore, the Hindus of Bangladesh have never been anything more than a group of sympathetic onlookers at best and a crowd of envious scoffers at worst. Today, as always, their attachment—mental, emotional, even physical —continues to be not with Bangladesh as such, but with the conceptual old Bengal and with India. And this truth is so self-evident that neither the Muslims of Bangladesh nor the Hindus themselves ever try to put a cover on it. The moment we take cognizance of this fundamental truth, all that the Hindu leaders of Bangladesh told this writer, and which has gone into record here through him, and all that they confided to him, but which has not been recorded here for reasons of propriety— both these categories of facts and opinions become at once simple, logical and easily understandable.

The explanation is that since the Hindus in Bangladesh are a minority and are destined to re-

main a minority as long as they live there, their
mental and emotional attachment to the greater
'Hindudom' of India cannot be snapped. It is
more or less the same position which the Muslims
occupy in India as a whole. Since the Muslims
in India are a minority and are destined to remain
so for ever, their emotional involvement with the
conceptual Islamic world outside, extending from
Pakistan to Morocco, cannot be put an end to.
There is indeed no need to do so, for to the extent
this involvement constitutes a 'Muslim bogey',
it helps in preventing the otherwise divisive Hindus
from falling apart. The only difference is that
while the Hindus of Bangladesh, or for that matter
in any other country of the world, are not obliged
to stay there under all circumstacnes—they can
always find a place in the lap of Mother India if
only they prepare themselves to forego wealth for
the sake of life and honour—the Muslims of India
have probably no other place to go in this entire,
wide world. The message of action contained in
this plain truth is for the Muslims themselves to
gauge and absorb.

But why do the Hindus of Bangladesh feel so
alienated from the 'national mainstream' in their
own 'country'? The reason is, again, the same which
is at the root of all the miseries of Indian Muslims,
especially in north India. It is a malady that can
be called 'morbid superiority complex'. It stems
from history and distorts the concept of nationalism
both for the Hindus of Bangladesh and the Muslims
of north India, inducing them to go on indulging
in dreams of having the upper hand. It makes the

Muslims of north India think of 'Indian Nationalism' only in terms of the social conditions that obtained in, say, the golden period of Mughal rule. So does it make the Hindus of Bangladesh think of their 'nationalism' only in terms of the social conditions that obtained under, say, the British. Of course, this feeling of superiority is only an internal, subjective state of mind; it has no relation to any reality. In the concrete and practical situation as it obtains, neither the Hindu in Bangladesh, nor the Muslim in North India, is of any account vis-a-vis the rest of the population.

In short, the definition of Bangladeshi nationalism as presented by Sheikh Mujib does not apply to his high-caste Hindu citizens. Rather, in a broad way, they come under the definition of 'Bengali' which we enunciated in the beginning of this discussion, and which is related to all Bengal and British India as they existed before Partition. Moreover, this other concept does not refer to any full-fledged nationalism either, because it has no history of a separate struggle for independence behind it. Thus it is clear that Sheikh Mujib's 'Bengali' and our 'Bengali' are two entirely different things. His 'Bengali' is a political entity and by religion is Muslim, whereas our 'Bengali' is a cultural entity and by religion is Hindu.

Only with this amendment or addition can we accept as correct the definition of Bangladeshi nationalism put forward by Sheikh Mujib. And as a corollary, therefore, what people like Professor Muzaffar Ahmed and Maulana Bhashani say on this subject is proved to be wrong. Hence, even if the

Maulana should live for another 90 years to carry
on his movement for greater Bengal, or some of the
romantic poets in our Bengal should go mad over
'Ma Bangla' in a million poems more, as long as the
two mutually hostile societies of the Hindus and
the Muslims exist intact in their respective ethos,
the dream of a united Bengal will never come true.
And if people should cease to think as Hindus and
Muslims, then, why united Bengal alone ? In that
case, the entire sub-continent is one.

Ever since the emergence of Bangladesh, even
the highest in our country have been shamelessly
claiming that the event has destroyed the two-nation
theory. Somebody should ask these hypocrites if
they could give one good reason for the separate
existence of Bangladesh after the destruction of the
two-nation theory. If the theory has been demo-
lished, as they claim, then the only logical conse-
quence should be the reunion of Bangladesh with
India, as seems to be the positive stand of the
Bangladeshi Hindus. Could these highly-placed
people, who are all the time drumming the false
news of the death of the two-nation theory, propose
to Sheikh Mujib that since the theory, on the strength
of which he had separated in 1947, exists no more,
his country had better revert to its old position of
subservience to Calcutta ? Perhaps these people
do not know, or perhaps they know it only too well,
that no person in Bangladesh today can dare to
assert from a public platform that what was done
in 1947 was wrong, for the people know that had
Pakistan not been created then, Bangladesh too
would not have come into existence now.

The truth is that even Sheikh Mujib himself does not use the term 'Bengali' in the same sense in which we use it in our Bengal. He does so only for convenience; that is, to avoid the longer and still somewhat unfamiliar term 'Bangladeshi'. What he means is that his people are 'Bengali' because they speak the Bengali language, nothing more than that. The Pakistanis, too, referred to the people of 'East Pakistan' as 'Bengalis' in the same sense; that is, in relation to their language only. But if a people had to be named only after the language they speak, then so many nations in the world would start having the same name that recognition would become a problem. Thus it is clear that the people of Bangladesh are also called 'Bengalis' only because of their language and nothing else. Actually, they are 'Bangladeshis ! And 'Bangladeshi' is an entirely new concept, discovered and adopted by the Muslims of East Bengal while living in Pakistan, just as the Hindus of Bengal had discovered and adopted the concept of being 'Bengali' while living in the British empire. The sense of being 'Bangladeshi' is, therefore, quite different from the sense of being 'Bengali'; the former is a recent product of Pakistani imperialism, while the latter is that of an older one—the British. It is presumably to maintain this difference that the Bangladesh Government enters in the nationality column of its passports, not 'Bengali' as used by Sheikh Mujib, but 'Bangladeshi'. That indeed is the correct form. For, whatever else the Bangladeshis may be—and they are better than many other South Asian nations—'Bengalis' they are definitely not.

Thus, once it is established that Bangladeshi nationalism is a cent per cent new and a cent per cent Muslim nationalism, it requires no clairvoyance to predict the future course of its evolution. Today in Bangladesh, the talk of a 'Bengali Muslim culture' is very much in the air. Erudite articles on the subject from the pens of renowned scholars are appearing in the local journals. But the truth is that, there is no such thing as a 'Bengali Muslim culture'. Of course, there is a Bengali culture, a very definite, well-organised and highly developed thing — but that culture is cent per cent Hindu. Even the solitary Kazi Nazarul Islam could step into it only to the extent he was prepared to sing eulogies to Kali and Krishna. This very culture is also a valued possession of the Hindus of Bangladesh. But so far as the Muslims are concerned—and they constitute the true Bangladeshis—the only culture they have so far been able to develop to a primitive level, is Agriculture !

The question is: what will the Bangladeshis do now ? On the one hand, in the name of Bengali culture, they will not find it easy to adopt the whole spectrum of thought and feeling from Raja Rammohan Roy to Swami Vivekananda; they will not be able to recreate the Vedic atmosphere of Shanti Niketan in their country. On the other hand, the old Pakistani humbug of false religiosity and pan-Islamic fanaticism too will never again raise its head in Bangladesh. If ever it does, it will be crushed at once by college students alone. As such, what exactly are they going to show to the world in the name of their high-sounding 'Bengali Muslim culture'?

The Bengali language ?   Well, to come down to
solid earth, the Bengali language is not *their* language;
they have used it only as a political weapon in their
fight against West Pakistani domination. With
its success, therefore, most of its utility value is
already over. It may remain a language of common discourse, even of administration at lower
levels. But pretty soon, its position is going to be
no different from that of our 'charkha'. Just as
the charkha utterly failed to meet most of the
demands of our economic life, so would the Bengali
language fail to meet the demands of the cultural
life of the Bangladeshis. To meet those demands,
as also to acquire all their standards and values
of worldly life, they would eventually and inevitably
have to look towards the same centres from which
all the Muslims of the sub-continent must derive
their cultural nourishment. These centres are in
India, and are linked in their historical background
with other centres outside India. An important
element in the heritage of these centres in India is
the Urdu language and all that it implies.

Therefore, at the clear risk of displeasing almost
everybody concerned, except perhaps the 'Pakistanis', both in India and Pakistan, this writer is
constrained, much against his own preferences but
for reasons of historical exactitude, to predict that
the Urdu language will be restored in Bangladesh
as the main vehicle of its cultural life, with Bengali
playing only second fiddle. He further predicts that
after the current problems between Bangladesh
and Pakistan are sorted out, and Pakistan formally
recognises Bangladesh and sets up its embassy in
Dacca, the elite and the common people of this

country will like to have the closest and most cordial relations with none but their erstwhile imperial masters. That will be the most natural thing to happen.

Sheikh Mujib may say for world consumption that he does not care for recognition by Pakistan, that more than one hundred countries have already recognised Bangladesh, etc. But he knows full well that the one thing his people are waiting for with bated breath is recognition by Pakistan. For, without this most important event taking place, they feel their independence to be incomplete and sovereignty doubtful. In fact, the day a Pakistani ambassador arrives in Dacca and presents his credentials to their President, will be a day of still greater rejoicing for the Bangladeshis than even their day of Independence. But, of course, for all these predictions to come true and stand th   of time, the Pakistani rulers, like the departe   sh before them, will have to acquire the under   ng and wisdom never to think of re-establish   eir rule over this former colony of theirs.